A
TRAVELLER'S
WINE GUIDE
TO

Spain

To Cándido Latorre and Miguel Merino,
two old friends from the Rioja

A
TRAVELLER'S
WINE GUIDE
TO

Spain

Desmond Begg

Foreword by Maria Isabel Mijares y Garcia-Pelayo

Photographs by Francesco Venturi

Aurum Press

The *Traveller's Wine Guides* were conceived and produced by Philip Clark Ltd, 53 Calton Avenue, London SE21 7DF, UK

Designed by Keith Faulkner Publishing Ltd

Edited by Philip Clark and Tony Raven

Photographs by Franceso Venturi (except where otherwise credited)

Maps by European Map Graphics Ltd, Andrew Green and Simon Green

Copyright © Philip Clark Ltd, 1989, 1998

First Edition published in 1989

This revised and updated edition published in 1998 by Aurum Press Ltd, 25 Bedford Avenue, London WC1B 3AT, UK

A catalogue record for this book is available from the British Library.

ISBN 1-85410-515-9

Printed in Singapore for Imago

ACKNOWLEDGMENTS

The author and publishers would particularly like to thank Charlotte Hey and María José Sevilla of **Wines from Spain** for all their help and support during the preparation of this book.

Philip Clark Ltd would also like to thank Keith Bambury for his help with the layouts, and Glen Keegan of Words & Pictures Ltd for his assistance with the cover design.

The many individuals and organizations who have provided help and information include Conchi Biurrun of Asociacion Exportadores de Vinos Navarra and Sonia Castro-Lanero of Bodegas Vilariño Cambados.

The maps of Navarra and Galicia, on pages 17 and 61 respectively, are based on originals kindly supplied by ICEX, Madrid.

COVER

Main illustration: The hilltop wine town of Laguardia, seen against the dramatic backdrop of the Sierra Cantabria, in the Rioja Alavesa.
(Photograph: Mick Rock/Cephas Picture Library)

Foreground photography by Darius

Road map of Spain: 1:800,000 courtesy of Ravenstein Verlag GmbH

TITLE ILLUSTRATION

Vines growing near the historic town of Cacabelos, in the Denomination of Origin of El Bierzo, the most westerly and one of the newest of Old Castile. Wine has been produced here since the Middle Ages.

(Photograph: Alan Williams)

PHOTO CREDITS

Antonio López Osés 41

Cephas Picture Library 21, 54, 62, 63, 119

Codorníu S.A., Spain 114

Robert Harding Picture Library Ltd 60, 93

The Sherry Institute of Spain 90/91

Alan Williams 37, 52, 84, 86, 92

Zefa Picture Library 125

Contents

How to Use this Book

This book is designed to give as much practical help to the serious wine traveller in Spain as possible.

Chapter by chapter, you are given an introduction to the different wine regions and cuisines of Spain, and are guided through the countryside to its best-known wineries and wine towns, as well as other historic sights and cities. Special advice about driving in Spain and about visiting bodegas can be found on pages 12 to 15, and general tourist information is given on pages 139 and 140. Sources of further information on wines appear on pages 138-9 and 141.

Each chapter has its regional map, showing its chief towns and sites of major wineries, and giving an outline of the road system. Further route maps of smaller areas are provided wherever necessary.

Information panels

Perhaps most useful to the tourist, however, are the information panels that accompany the text as it guides you through the individual regions. These panels will give you a clear idea of the range of bodegas that can be visited, their opening times, their facilities, and additional points of interest (such as architecture or history). The symbols used are shown in the panel (above right). The panels also include details on wine museums, some recommended wine shops and restaurants, occasional special food markets, and a useful selection of state-run hotels or Paradors.

The bodegas

Although the selection of bodegas is wide, it does not include every Spanish bodega that is open to the public. This book concentrates on those that – in the author's opinion –

are worth visiting, either because their wines are outstanding or because their wineries are most touristically attractive.

If a reservation is necessary, it is best to contact the bodega well in advance, by letter (a sample letter in Spanish is given in the Reference Section, on page 140) – and then phone within one or two days of your intended visit to confirm the arrangement (advice on how to use the telephone in Spain is provided on page 140). Most bodegas offer a free tasting, but a purchase of wine, however small, will be much appreciated.

Restaurants

Again, the recommended restaurants are a selection, since it is not possible to give details of all the good restaurants in Spain within the scope of this book. *Recommendations are made on the grounds of quality alone.* Some of them will be expensive, so it is worth checking the menu displayed outside before you enter the premises.

Further guidance on restaurants can be found in books recommended on page 141. A reservation, incidentally, is usually recommended on Sundays and in the evenings, particularly in the cities.

Wine shops

Wine retailing in Spain is still considerably under-developed, and there are few specialist shops. Those that are listed are highly recommended, not only because of their selection of fine wines but because you can be confident that the wines have been properly handled and cellared. Other non-specialist shops are also worth browsing in, especially for local curiosities, but their storage conditions may not always be ideal.

INFORMATION PANEL SYMBOLS	
E	English spoken
F	French spoken
G	German spoken
I	Italian spoken
TF	Tastings are free
TP	Tastings must be paid for
WS	Wine for sale
☎	Telephoning/faxing in advance advisable
☎	Appointment must be made in advance by telephone or fax
Av.	Avenida (Avenue)
Clle.	Calle (Street)
Ctra.	Carretera (Road)
Pl.	Plaza (Square)
s/n	*sin número* (no number)

Foreword

Spain is a country with a centuries-old tradition of winemaking, and wine has played a special part in the country's history on numerous occasions.

Some 1,600,000 hectares (four million acres) of vineyards, distributed throughout the length and breadth of the country, produce a wide range of wines, each with its own special characteristics. Different climatic conditions; soils with different structures, textures and depths; different varieties of grapes; and the technologies used in the production and ageing of the wines – all of these are factors which have made their contribution to wines that are justifiably famous throughout the world.

In recent years, major technological improvements in most of the country's wine regions have also ensured that more modern and elegant wines are now being produced, better adapted to the taste of the new consumer. These trends are not confined to the well-known traditional regions such as Jerez, the Rioja and Valdepeñas. New regions with high quality wines, such as Somontano and the Ribera del Duero, are also emerging.

This great diversity of wines, coupled with the variety of cuisines that can be found in the different regions, is one of the great attractions for the traveller in Spain. Those who make their journey through the country's varied regions, discovering the many reminders of its colourful history as well as the modern face of Spain, will find in its wines a living symbol of a unique civilization and culture.

Maria Isabel Mijares y Garcia-Pelayo
Secretaire General de l'Union Internationale des Oenologues

Introduction

Spain is no longer on the periphery of Europe, and is now a valued member of the European Union, respected for the social and economic progress it has achieved over the past twenty years. Unsurprisingly, the Spaniards have rediscovered a pride in all things Spanish: their rich and varied culture; their exuberant lifestyle; and their internationally acclaimed fashion industry and cuisine.

The Spanish have also looked outward to the rest of the world, and foreign influence on all aspects of their life is far greater than it has ever been. The wine industry too has looked abroad, and borrowed grape varieties and technology to enhance the quality of its wines, while still maintaining their unique character.

Away from the crowded Costas, Spain remains a fascinating country of historic cities, high mountain ranges and wide plateaus. Most of its wine regions are in the interior, in unspoiled countryside far from the coastal belt.

A wine tour of Spain, therefore, will reveal a range of cultural and gastronomic experiences that few visitors knew existed, and will help the wine traveller to get to the heart of this largely unknown country.

This book outlines two basic routes that lead from north to south through Spain's wine regions. The first begins at the western end of the Pyrenees and leads you through the interior, from Navarra, into the Rioja, then Old and New Castile, ending in the southern region of Andalusia. The second route is simpler, following the Mediterranean coast from the French border southward to Alicante, passing through Catalonia and the Levante district.

Within each region, a special wine route is suggested. And there are two further forays included: one into Galicia from either the Rioja or Old Castile; and another into Aragon from either the Rioja or Catalonia.

The Grand Tour

For the determined traveller, a full tour will take some weeks. You can complete one of the north–south tours, either the inland or the coastal route, and then follow the second one in reverse on the return journey. To enjoy this to the full, however, you will need plenty of stamina as well as time.

Shorter visits

If you are planning a shorter visit, there are a number of alternatives. One is a tour covering only the northern regions, travelling through Navarra, the Rioja, Aragon and Catalonia. Or, a longer journey can lead through Navarra, the Rioja, the Castiles, the Levante and Catalonia, ending once again at the French border. But these routes have the disadvantage that they miss out the regions of the South.

Another visit could be dedicated to Andalusia – a large and fascinating province, with enough interest to merit an individual tour. Whichever route you choose, you are likely to be tempted into another. Few tourists can exhaust the attractions in just one trip.

BAY OF
BISCAY

FRANCE

ASTURIAS Santander Bilbao Pamplona
BASQUE NAVARRA
Santiago de Compostela COUNTRY Huesca CATALONIA
GALICIA Logroño Barcelona
THE RIOJA Lérida
OLD CASTILE R. Ebro
Valladolid Zaragoza Tarragona
R. Duero ARAGON
Zamora
Segovia
PORTUGAL Madrid
THE Palma de Mallorca
LEVANTE MENORCA
R. Tagus NEW CASTILE Valencia THE BALEARICS
Alcázar de San Juan MALLORCA
EXTREMADURA R. Júcar IBIZA
Valdepeñas MURCIA
R. Guadiana Alicante MEDITERRANEAN
R. Segura SEA
R. Guadalquivir
Córdoba
Sevilie ANDALUSIA
Granada
Málaga
Jerez

CANARY ISLANDS

LA PALMA LANZAROTE
TENERIFE Santa Cruz FUERTEVENTURA
LA GOMERA Las Palmas
HIERRO GRAN CANARIA
MOROCCO

The System of Classification

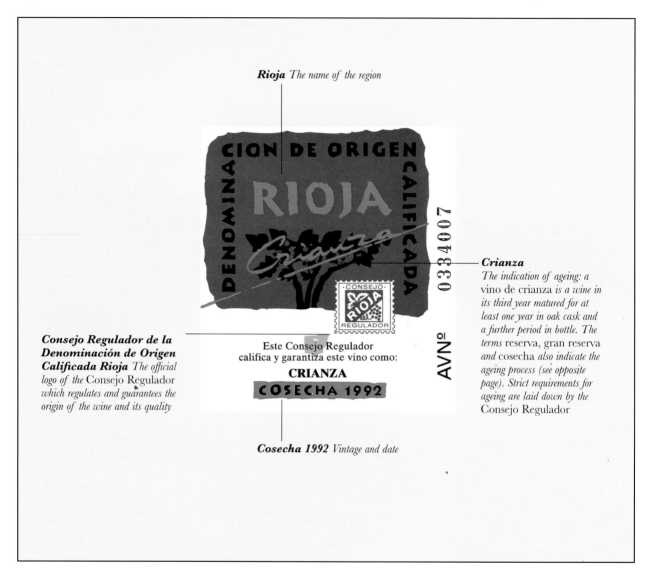

Rioja *The name of the region*

Crianza
The indication of ageing: a vino de crianza *is a wine in its third year matured for at least one year in oak cask and a further period in bottle. The terms* reserva, gran reserva *and* cosecha *also indicate the ageing process (see opposite page). Strict requirements for ageing are laid down by the* Consejo Regulador

Consejo Regulador de la Denominación de Origen Calificada Rioja *The official logo of the* Consejo Regulador *which regulates and guarantees the origin of the wine and its quality*

Este Consejo Regulador califica y garantiza este vino como:
CRIANZA
COSECHA 1992

Cosecha 1992 *Vintage and date*

The need for classification

Despite producing less wine than either Italy or France, Spain has more land under vine than any other country in the world. Its climate varies considerably from the north, where the influence of the Atlantic predominates, to the regions of the south and east, which are more Mediterranean in character, and the result is a wide variety of types of wines.

Although the progress achieved by Spain's wine industry has been impressive in recent years, it has also been uneven, with the production and ageing facilities of some regions lagging well behind those of others. To hasten improvements, the Spanish authorities, encouraged by the European Union, have created an official system to guarantee the consumer a minimum level of quality and give him or her some guidance.

A gran reserva (far left) is a wine made from a great vintage that has been aged for at least three years in oak cask and three in bottle.

A reserva (left) is a selected wine that has been aged for at least three years, at least one of which must have been in cask.

Wines with little or no ageing usually have the word cosecha *(vintage) followed by a date only.*

*The letters C.V.C. (*Contiene Varias Cosechas*), now only rarely encountered, mean that the wine is a blend of several vintages.*

The Denominations of Origin

Central to this system are the *Denominaciónes de Origen* or Denominations of Origin (D.O.s), similar to the French *Appellations Contrôlées* or Italian *Denominazioni di Origine*. In 1996 there were 49 of these dotted around the country, each overseen by a *Consejo Regulador* (C.R.) or Regulating Council.

As the regions' quality watchdogs, these *Consejos* oversee virtually every aspect of wine production and ageing: they ensure that the wine is made from grapes grown within the delimited area; that it is made from authorized varieties; and that the wineries in which it is made are suitably equipped and maintain a high standard of cleanliness and hygiene.

Furthermore, every year the *Consejos* reject any parcel of wine that they do not consider to be of sufficient quality, which is then either sold off in bulk or distilled. These standards are exacting. But every bottle that meets them is then entitled to the coveted label on the back of every D.O. wine.

The back label

The back label also gives the consumer an indication of the ageing that the wine has undergone. In general Spanish wines are divided into *vino del año*, *crianzas*, *reservas* or *gran reservas* depending on how much ageing they have been given in barrel and bottle.

There are, of course some fine wines that are produced outside the D.O. network and which are not entitled to a *Consejo* back label. But, most of the time, an official back label is the consumer's best guarantee of reliability and quality.

Driving in Spain

There are three main points to keep in mind if you are driving in Spain. First, Spain does not have a brilliant safety record. For example, there are more than twice the number of road deaths in Spain than in the U.K. This may compare favourably with some other European countries, but it is a sobering statistic. Secondly, Spanish drink-driving laws, although strict on paper, are lax in practice, and it is still quite common to see roadside cafés at lunchtime packed with lorry drivers drinking wine and brandy. Thirdly, Spain is one of the most mountainous countries in Europe, so driving here can be hazardous.

Obviously, you must always drive with care. Here are a few tips:
* remember to drive on the right, and give way to traffic from the right.

Contrasting landscapes. Varieties planted in the cool northern regions (above) include classic French grapes. The southern vineyards (right) produce the famous fortified wines.

* seatbelts are compulsory outside town or city boundaries.
* you must have a regulation sticker (eg **G.B.**) on a properly registered car
* carry a breakdown triangle.
* always carry a spare tyre and a jack, a spare set of headlight bulbs, and a reserve of oil, water and petrol. (Petrol stations and garages are scarce in remoter regions.)
* make sure you are well insured.
* last but by no means least, do not get tempted into prolonged lunchtime drinking or tastings if you have to drive afterwards.

The roads

The **nacionales** are the main thoroughfares in Spain and are usually crowded. In particular, they are used by most of the big lorries, which can make for frustrating driving, especially in mountainous areas.

The **autopistas** carry comparatively light traffic, as they have tolls, but they make long journeys comfortable, and their service areas are usually excellent. The *autopistas* are a good way to bypass large cities.

Lower in rank are the C roads which link towns in rural areas. These are generally narrow and vary in quality from good to appalling (hence the possible need for spare tyres).

Signposts for the *autopistas* are in white letters on a blue background, as opposed to those of the *nacionales* and C roads, which have black letters on a white background.

SPEED LIMITS
Urban areas 50 km/h (31 mph)
Normal roads 90–100 km/h (56–62 mph)
Motorways 120 km/h (74mph)

ALCOHOL LIMIT
80mg per 100ml of blood

PETROL
CAMPSA, the national petrol distribution company, sells the following grades:
Standard (gasolina) 90 octane
Super 96 octane
Extra 98 octane
Sin Plomo unleaded

DOCUMENTS
You should keep your passport and driving licence with you at all times.

INSURANCE
Consult your motoring organization or insurance company. To be on the safe side it is worth getting a Green Card and increasing your insurance cover (for yourself and for any passengers). The costs of litigation in Spain are high.

DRIVING TIPS
* To avoid traffic jams, don't drive into cities on Sunday nights or out of them on Sunday mornings.
* Never leave your car unlocked, and don't leave valuables in view. If possible, use hotel car parks, or guarded ones.
* Truck drivers indicate right when it is safe to overtake. If they then indicate left or stop indicating, there is oncoming traffic.
* Remember that it is compulsory to carry a spare set of headlight bulbs.

Visiting a Bodega

Bodegas and co-operatives

Among the best welcomes in Spain are to be found in Jerez in the far south corner. As you drive into the town you are greeted by billboards inviting you to visit the sherry bodegas. Most of the leading firms have guided tours of their premises which end with a tasting and usually include a video on sherry production.

But Jerez is the exception rather than the rule. In general the Spanish wine industry has not yet woken up to wine tourism. Comparatively few of its bodegas are prepared to give tours of their premises (though membership of a wine club or a wine appreciation circle will certainly help you), and many do not even sell wine on the premises.

Unfortunately, this means that you will not find an automatic welcome from all of the companies which rate a mention in this book. Their wines, however, will almost always be available in local restaurants and wine shops.

Fortunately, the co-operatives are usually hospitable. They may not be the most exciting wineries, but they are mainly more than willing to give tastings and to sell wine to the passer-by. Once you are on their premises, it may be fairly easy to persuade them to conduct a short tour.

Prior reservations

Those other companies that are open to the public are listed with relevant information in the data panels in

Different regions of Spain have their traditional styles of bodega architecture. The cellars of Gonzalez Byass in Jerez, with their whitewashed walls covered in must, and their old wooden butts full of ageing wine, are typically Andalusian in character and are a testimony to centuries of sherry-producing tradition.

each section, along with recommended wine shops and restaurants. In most cases it is necessary to book in advance. If you decide to do this by letter or fax, you should leave plenty of time for a reply. An extended trip around the wine regions of Spain needs and deserves this careful planning.

These visits are nearly always well worth the extra effort. The Spanish are very hospitable, and if you have taken the trouble to write or telephone in advance you will be greeted with characteristic courtesy.

So, if you make an appointment, do be sure to honour it. And, if you are delayed along the way, do telephone your hosts if you can (see the section on using the telephone in Spain, and a sample letter, on page 140).

There is an added bonus to most bodega visits. There are many styles of winery – for example, the bodegas of Andalusia are very different from those of Catalonia. And, while some companies have made great efforts to keep up with modern viniculture, others maintain an unshakeable loyalty to tradition.

In contrast to the traditional bodega architecture of Andalusia, the wineries of Catalonia are often highly modernized, making full use of advanced technology. The stainless steel fermentation tanks shown above belong to the Codorníu winery in Sant Sadurní d'Anoia.

Navarra

N avarra, as the traveller will soon discover, is a region that is steeped in history. From the moment that you cross the border, preferably through the historic Pyrenean pass of Roncesvalles made famous by the *Song of Roland*, you become aware of an active, restless and war-torn past.

Navarra was formerly a proud, independent kingdom which reached the zenith of its power in the 11th century, when it stretched to Bordeaux in the north and Barcelona in the east. It has witnessed, and suffered, a constant ebb and flow of conquering or retreating armies from the time of the Moors, forced southward by Charlemagne, to the Civil War, when Carlist volunteers rallied in their thousands to the Nationalist cause.

On a more peaceful note, the northern part of the province is crossed by the route to Santiago de Compostela, and its numerous chapels and churches are a testimony to the pilgrims.

Today Navarra is a prosperous province producing excellent meat and vegetables as well as wine. Its countryside has often been described as a microcosm of Spain, with the Pyrenean hills of the north giving way to the flat, dry plains of the south.

To get to Pamplona
Pamplona is 160km (100 miles) south of Bilbao along the N240 (no tolls) and the A15 (tolls); it is 80km (50 miles) north of Logroño along the N111 (no tolls); 430km (270 miles) north-east of Madrid along the N1 to Burgos, the N120 to Logroño and the N111 (no tolls); or 480km (300 miles) via the N1 to Burgos, the A1 and A68 (tolls), and the N111 (no tolls).

A trout-filled river flows through the small town of Sumbilla in the Pyrenean north of Navarra.

The point of departure for the wine traveller is the ancient and historic city of Pamplona, which can be reached from France by one of two routes. You can drive along the C133 which becomes the N121 and branches off from the Al *autopista* (the continuation of the French A63) at the border. Devotees of history may, however, wish to follow the more rugged Pyrenean C135 which begins at the mountain pass of Roncesvalles close to the French towns of Valcarlos and St Jean-Pied-de-Port.

If you rent a car at Bilbao, you will have to circle the city on the motorway ring roads and leave on the A68 *autopista* which rises to the high Puerto de Altube. Then take the turning to Vitoria and follow the well-signposted N1 and N240. Those arriving on the Santander ferry should take the route to Bilbao and then follow the same instructions.

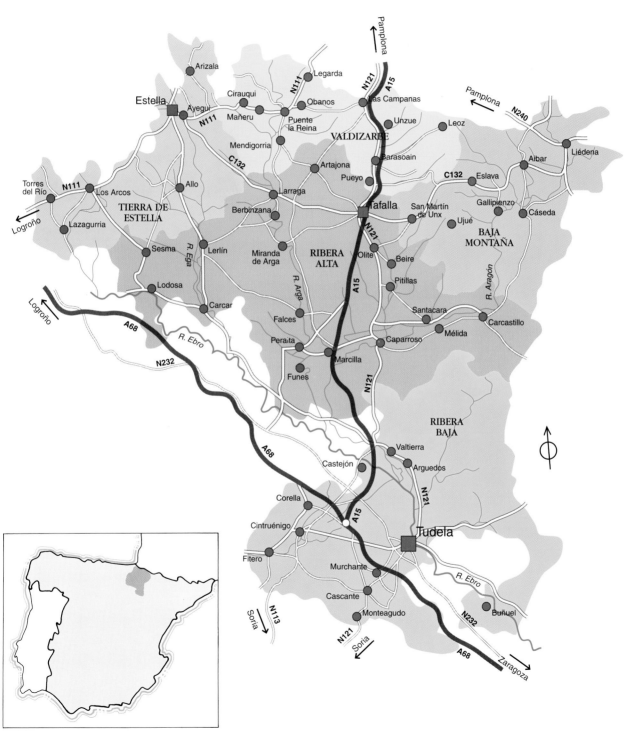

The Wines of Navarra

The Denomination of Origin of Navarra covers some 17,000 hectares (42,000 acres) of vineyards between Pamplona and the great Ebro river. It is divided into five sub-regions: the Valdizarbe around Puente la Reina; the Baja Montaña on the border with Aragon to the east; the Tierra Estella around the town of Estella; the Ribera Alta around Olite; and the Ribera Baja around Cintruénigo and Tudela.

The altitude drops as you move south, leading to higher temperatures and lower rainfall. The region produces about 60 million litres (about 13 million Imperial gallons/16 million US gallons) of wine a year with a guarantee of origin.

Grape varieties
Despite recent progress, the Garnacha is still Navarra's leading grape variety, covering some 67 per cent of the entire vineyard area. There are, however, increased plantings of other varieties, especially Tempranillo, Cabernet Sauvignon, Chardonnay and Viura on the higher ground of the Tierra de Estella and the Ribera Alta.

Navarra is being increasingly described as the most exciting Spanish wine region of the 1990s and there is no doubt that its progress in the last 15 years has been impressive. During this period, a rising flow of high quality reds and whites has been added to its already well established range of *rosados* (rosés or pink wines). This development has enabled it to shake off its one-dimensional, one-colour image – and has brought its dream of being accepted as one of Spain's greatest wine regions that much closer.

Navarra's reputation was initially built on the quality of its *rosados*. The basis of this quality was the character of the much-maligned but frequently planted Garnacha grape, which thrives in the region's climate. When picked early and macerated for only a short time to extract just the right amount of colour from the skin, there can be little doubt that it produces some of the very best *rosados* in Spain – dark pink in colour, fruity and quite high in alcohol (12–13 per cent). More importantly, they are dry – very much drier than those made in other parts of Europe, with more body, structure and complexity. Those that are aged in wood have interesting brick-yellow colour overtones and a subtle touch of oak.

In Spain their popularity was such that, while in the 1970s they accounted for only 25 per cent of the region's

The 16th-century fortress of the kings of Navarra with its 15 towers dominates Olite, unofficial capital of the region's wine country and seat of its highly regarded enological station EVENA. Ochoa wines illustrate the fortress on their labels.

production, by the mid-1980s this percentage had grown to over half.

From the mid-1980s, however, the region changed its focus. Inspired by the phenomenal success of Rioja on foreign markets, Navarra embarked on a revolution that has transformed its wine industry. With plenty of support and encouragement from the provincial government, an impressive programme of investment in wineries and vineyards was launched, and the spectacular results are only now coming on to international markets.

The region's vinicultural base was the first to benefit. All over the region new, lighter crushers were installed. Stainless steel tanks for temperature-controlled fermentations rose like giants in the region's wineries. New barrels of American and French oak were stacked up in its ageing halls.

By the beginning of the 1990s, much had been achieved. The region's whites had got fruitier and crisper as a result of better, more controlled fermentation. More well-made and carefully-aged *crianzas* and even *reservas* began to appear. Even the famous *rosados* improved as a result of better vinification.

The second part of the revolution took longer to bear fruit. While the wineries were being renovated, work was also going on in the vineyards. Any grower willing to replant his vineyards with grape varieties approved by the *Consejo Regulador* qualified for cheap loans from the provincial government. The result was that plantings of Tempranillo, Viura and even Cabernet Sauvignon and Chardonnay slowly began to increase. These, like all vineyards, took time to come to maturity. But they are now on stream, giving the more adventurous producers a steady flow of high quality wine from several different varieties with which to experiment.

Blends of Chardonnay with Viura, of Garnacha, Tempranillo and Cabernet are now being made more frequently. More experimentation is being carried out with barrel fermentation and different periods of ageing. The range of Navarra's wines, as well as their quality, has improved immeasurably, and there can be little doubt that wine-making here will continue to progress: it is still clearly a region to watch.

Most of the leading producers welcome visitors and are listed in the panels. There are two, however, that are not, the first because it does not accept visitors and the second because a visit to its winery involves a significant detour. So, look out for the wines of Ochoa and Bodegas Principe de Viana – as they are well worth tasting.

Much of the winery of Vinícola Navarra in Las Campanas (see page 21) dates back to 1850. The company is now a leading wine producer in the region. The recently installed high-technology equipment here contrasts with the old bodegas.

Pamplona

PAMPLONA

RECOMMENDED WINE SHOPS
Casa Chavez Sancho el
Fuerte 8.
Museo del Vino Sancho
el Fuerte 77.
   Both conveniently
located on the same street,
they offer a wide selection
from all regions of Spain.

**RECOMMENDED
RESTAURANTS**
Hartza Juan de Labrit 19.
Tel: 22 45 68.
Alhambra Francisco
Bergamin 7. Tel: 24 50 07.
Rodero Emilio Arrieta 3.
Tel: 22 80 35.

Pamplona, as any reader of
Hemingway will tell you, is best
known in Spain for the *Feria de San
Fermín*, the famous bullfighting fiesta
in July.

   Behind this flamboyant reputation,
however, lies a pulsating and
increasingly sophisticated regional
capital with a compact centre of
narrow streets flanked by tall, old
houses and more open modern
districts of wide avenues. It has an
interesting Gothic cathedral,
attractive gardens, an impressive
central fort, the *Ciudadela*, and an
interesting covered market.

   Pamplona is neither a gastronomic
nor a wine centre, and has no

bodegas. Its chief attraction to the
wine traveller is that, in its
restaurants, bars and shops, you can
find the greatest range of regional
wines available. The city gives the
visitor an opportunity to become
acquainted with the wines and
cuisine of the region before
embarking on a tour.

   Three good restaurants are listed
here (left), but those looking for local
colour are recommended to stroll the
streets of the centre and, after an
apéritif, to eat in one of the city's
lively and unpretentious *asadores*.
These are roasting houses where
enormous portions of meat are grilled
on an open fire and served with salad
or other vegetables.

   If you ask for the house wine, it
will be served in an earthenware jar
and will usually be rough and ready.
The wines of the leading firms in the
region will, however, also be
represented on the wine list. The
bigger restaurants usually offer a
greater selection, which will not be
restricted to the wines of the region.

   The city has several good hotels in
the centre. Parking can be difficult
despite the large car park near the
Avenida del Ejército.

*Graffiti adorns the bust of the American author
Ernest Hemingway that stands outside the bullring
in Pamplona and commemorates his frequent visits
to the* Feria de San Fermín.

Navarra's Wine Country

The wine country of Navarra begins immediately to the south of Pamplona. It is best to leave the city by the busy N121 in the direction of Tudela, the province's second city.

First stop is at the town of Las Campanas some 15km (9 miles) from Pamplona, the home of Vinícola Navarra, which stands on the left-hand side of the road. The winery, owned by one of Spain's largest wine companies, contains state-of-the-art wine-making equipment, but is housed in buildings dating back to 1850 that have been carefully restored. In a way, the company symbolizes Navarra itself, with its traditions and new developments.

Puente la Reina

Just on the other side of the town, a turning to the west will lead you through hilly country dotted with vineyards and asparagus to Puente la Reina. This was the junction of the pilgrim routes which entered Spain through the passes of Somport and Roncesvalles, and there is a statue of a pilgrim at the entrance to the town.

The huge Señorío de Sarría, a mixed farm complete with workers' village, and one of the region's most famous wine producers, lies on the outskirts. It is approached through a forest with occasional glimpses of the river and certainly justifies a visit.

LAS CAMPANAS
Vinícola Navarra Ctra. Pamplona-Zaragoza Km.14, Las Campanas. Tel: 36 01 31. Fax: 36 02 75. (Eduardo Sainz Amillo). Mon-Fri 0900-1400. Closed Aug. Modern winery housed in 19th-century buildings. E.F.TF.WS. ☎

PUENTE LA REINA
Bodegas de Sarría
Puente la Reina. Tel: 26 75 62. Fax: 17 21 64. (Pedro Catalán, Heli Crespo). Mon-Fri 1000-1200. Closed Jul-Oct. English-speaking tours sometimes available through prior arrangement. TF.WS. ☎ (Telephone above number in Pamplona several days before your visit.)

RECOMMENDED RESTAURANT
Mesón del Peregrino
Ctra. Logroño-Pamplona Km.23. Tel: 34 00 75. One of the most beautiful restaurants of Navarra.

The Señorío de Sarría estate lies just outside Puente la Reina. The approach road runs through a forest, through which the river Arga can be glimpsed.

Puente la Reina has witnessed the tramp of countless pilgrims over the hump-backed bridge that crosses the Arga river.

Estella

A few kilometres to the south of Puente la Reina on the N111 you come to Estella, also on the pilgrim route to Santiago. The fascinating architecture of this small town, built on both banks of the Ega river, includes the old palace of the Kings of Navarra. In the 19th century the palace became the headquarters of the Carlists, the supporters of Don Carlos de Borbón, Pretender to the Spanish throne.

Across the river, in the neighbouring hamlet of Ayegui, is the monastery of Irache, another stop on the pilgrim route. In the 16th century the monastery became a Benedictine university.

Next door you will find Bodegas Irache, one of the region's leading wineries. A visit to both is a rewarding experience.

Tafalla, Ujué and Olite

From Ayegui it is necessary to double back along the N111 for a short way and then take the narrow, rugged C132 that leads to Tafalla. This is a small, rather dull town but has an excellent restaurant, the Tubal.

If you are not yet hungry, take the small road that leads up to Ujué, a high, picturesque town with fabulous views, a fortress and a Romanesque church. Have lunch or dinner at the highly recommended Mesón las Torres – then double back to Tafalla and then head south along the N121 to Olite. This is the unofficial capital of the region's wine industry and seat of EVENA, its highly rated enological station (centre of wine studies). The town is overshadowed by its great fortress, with its massive ramparts and 15 towers, originally built in the 16th century by Charles the Noble. As part of this monument has been converted into a comfortable Parador Nacional, it is an ideal overnight stop. Do not miss Casa Zanito, an excellent restaurant.

Tudela

From Olite follow the N121 south. There is an interesting detour to the well-signposted Cistercian monastery of La Oliva built in the 11th and 12th centuries. Otherwise continue south and then south-east to Tudela – a fascinating town with a splendid cathedral and several interesting palaces.

Cascante

Cascante is a short distance away on the N121. The town has a fine basilica and parish church and is the home of Bodegas Guelbenzu, one of the most dynamic wine firms of Navarra. Until recently, Guelbenzu sold its wines in bulk for export, but it is now in the vanguard of the region's wine revolution.

The bodega occupies the basement and first floor of the house belonging to the family that owns it, and is surrounded by gardens bursting with flowers and trees. So visit the winery, have a tasting and then take a stroll around the grounds.

Cintruénigo

The last stop in our tour of Navarra is Cintruénigo, not far away. Go back along the N121 and branch off westwards to Murchante. Cintruénigo is the next town.

Bodegas Julián Chivite is another family-owned company and, as Navarra's largest, is on a different scale. But do not be deceived by its size; it is one of the most innovative and prestigious of the region and the

winery, with its oak barrels, cooperage and modern fermentation equipment is a testimony to the commitment of three generations of the family to the production of fine wine. A short walk away is Maher, a very good Michelin-starred restaurant.

Further travel

Cintruénigo is a mere 20-minute drive from Alfaro, the first town in the Rioja Baja. Alternatively, the N232 leads to the Denomination of Campo de Borja in Aragon.

At Julián Chivite's winery at Cintruénigo, fermentation takes place in temperature-controlled stainless steel tanks.

Food and Festivals of Navarra

FOOD SPECIALITIES

Bacalao al Ajoarriero There are many very sophisticated variations to this traditional dish. It comes from the northern part of the region and used to be served to *arrieros* (muleteers) at roadside inns in the evening. The traditional version combines salt cod from the Basque coast with garlic, peppers and sometimes tomatoes and onions. In leading restaurants, prawns, crayfish and even lobster are added.

Trucha a la Navarra Fried trout, often stuffed with ham and served with mushrooms, garlic and parsley.

Caldereta Ribereña As this is a peasant dish from the South of the province, the ingredients tend to vary. Basically, it is a stew made with whatever the cook has to hand.

Cordero en Chilindrón Although roast lamb is as popular in Navarra as it is throughout northern Spain, this is a typical and delicious alternative. The lamb is cooked with slices of ham and a sauce of garlic, onions, tomatoes and, of course, the famous red peppers. A variation is *Pimientos en Chilindrón* with large slices of peppers used instead of the lamb.

Perdiz a la Tudelana As its name implies, this is a dish from the southern part of the province. Partridges are cooked with quartered apples and served with boiled potatoes and mushrooms.

Festoons of chorizo sausages, a speciality of Navarra, hang in the shops and market stalls of Navarran towns along with the black morcilla sausage, often richly flavoured with cinnamon, pine nuts and raisins.

FESTIVALS

Curiously, Navarra has no big wine fair. Virtually every town in the wine country celebrates the end of the *vendimia* (the grape harvest) in September or October, but here there is nothing to compare to San Mateo in Logroño or the *Feria de la Vendimia* in Jerez.

Despite this, Navarra has a fiesta which is like no other. Every year, in early July, Pamplona takes a break and explodes into an almost unbelievable week of 'running the bulls', drinking, eating and dancing to celebrate the feast of the city's patron saint. However politicized and commercial the *Feria de San Fermín* has become, there can be little doubt that it remains one of the greatest and most exhilarating fiestas in Europe, if not in the world. If you want to take part, make sure that you book your hotel room well in advance.

NAVARRA'S CUISINE

Many of the great dishes of Navarra are also typical of Rioja and Aragon. *Menestra de Verduras* and the *chilindrón* sauce, for example, can be found in all three regions. In fact, the three provinces are inter-related in many ways, historically and culturally, and it is not surprising that their regional cuisines bear a family likeness. But in general, perhaps because of its more varied climate, it is Navarra that offers the greatest diversity.

Mushrooms, trout and game

The province's cooks have an excellent range of local ingredients at their disposal. Wild mushrooms grow in abundance, mostly in the north, and their sublime flavour can best be appreciated in the famous *Revuelto de setas* where they are combined with beaten eggs and garlic.

The north also produces from its mountain streams a wealth of trout, which are the centrepiece of the province's most famous dish, *Trucha a la Navarra*. There are also small game birds, particularly quail (*codornices*) and partridges (*perdices*), prepared in a variety of ways, with vegetables, wine and even with bitter chocolate.

Artichokes, asparagus, peppers

The southern part of the province, and particularly the Ribera region on the banks of the Ebro, is famous for its vegetables, and vegetable patches are often a feature of the landscape, especially the bright green clumps of asparagus fern.

The artichokes and asparagus from the region are delicious. They are usually served as entrées with either mayonnaise or vinaigrette.

This area is also the home of what are generally regarded as the best red peppers of the country, the *pimientos del piquillo*, so-called because of their beak-shaped ends. These are usually fried, to accompany grilled meat, stuffed with a variety of different ingredients, or made into the famous *chilindrón* sauce which accompanies two other very typical Navarra dishes, the *Cordero* (roast lamb) or the *Pimientos en Chilindrón* (see opposite page).

A visit to the covered market in Pamplona will reveal a splendid display of local products, ranging from fish and game to the region's vegetables.

The Rioja

W ith its powerful agricultural base, the Rioja is one of the richest provinces of Spain, producing some of the finest vegetables in the country as well as famous wines. Its wine production may be small when compared to that of other regions such as La Mancha or Valencia, but it is still Spain's premier table-wine producer.

This is also a congenial region to visit, since eating and drinking are taken seriously and the hospitality of the people is legendary. The landscape offers a contrast between the flat plains of the Rioja Baja and the more rugged terrain of the Alta and Alavesa, both of which are overshadowed by the brooding mountains of the Sierra de Cantabria.

RIOJA – THE GRAPES

With vineyards in three provinces – the Rioja itself, Navarra and Alava – the demarcated wine region of the Rioja is divided into three zones: the Rioja Baja, to the south and east; the Rioja Alavesa to the north of the Ebro; and the Rioja Alta to the west of Logroño.

Because of different soils and climates and the predominance of different grape varieties, these three sub-regions produce red wines that are very different in style: the Baja, where the Garnacha predominates, tends to produce open, fruity wines with good colour and high in alcohol. The Alta and the Alavesa, where the Tempranillo is king, produce leaner, less luscious wines but with greater aroma, elegance and acidity to help them improve during long periods of barrel ageing.

Although there are some wines produced using grapes from only one sub-region, usually the Alta or the Alavesa, most Riojas are blends of wines from the three zones.

The route

Because the N232 and the A68 flow through the region from south-east to north-west like vital arteries, the wine route is comparatively straightforward.

The Rioja Baja

From Cintruénigo and Corella, where the tour of Navarra ends, it is a short drive along local roads to Alfaro, the first wine town of the Rioja Baja (or Low Rioja). From there it is about 20km (12 miles) to the larger town of Calahorra where detours can he taken to Arnedo, Quel and Grávalos. From there you can approach Logroño, via the N232 or the A68.

The Rioja Alavesa

Fuenmayor, the first wine town of the Rioja Alta (or High Rioja), is a mere 10km (6 miles) further up the N232. Here a small country road leads northward into the Rioja Alavesa and the town of Laguardia with its wineries at the foot of the Sierra de Cantabria. You then drive down again along a similar road to the town of Elciego, the birthplace of the modern Riojan wine industry.

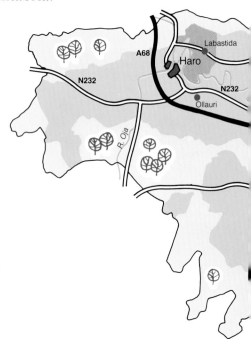

The Rioja Alta

From Elciego it is another short but scenic hop down the N232 to Cenicero, our second town in the Alta, and then another 30km (19 miles) to Haro, with an interesting detour to Paternina cellars at the hamlet of Ollauri on the way.

The Iregua river valley is typical of the rugged terrain of the Rioja Alta.

To get to Logroño
Logroño is 130km (88miles) S of Bilbao on the A68; 350km (217miles) NE of Madrid on the N1 to Burgos, then the N120 (no tolls), or 400km (250miles) via the N1 to Burgos and the Al and A68 (tolls).

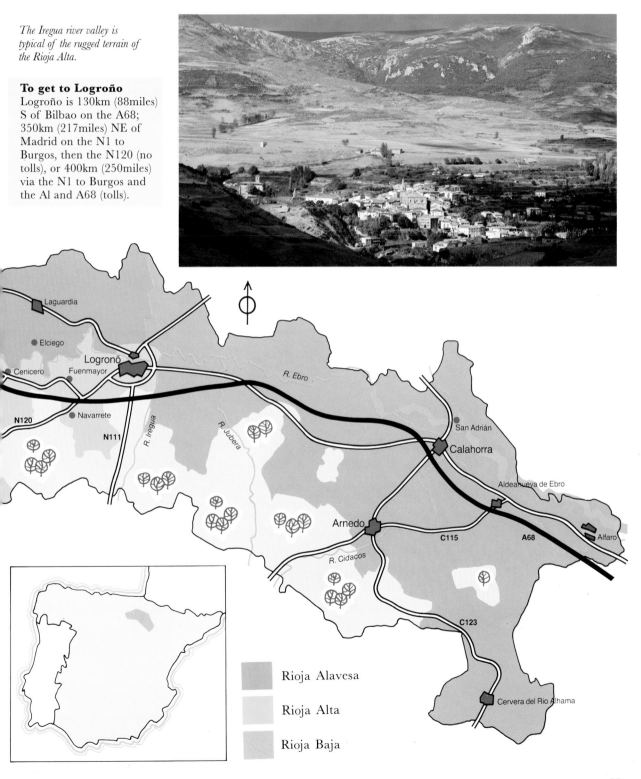

Laguardia

Elciego

Logroño

Cenicero

Fuenmayor

N120

Navarrete

N111

R. Iregua

R. Jubera

R. Ebro

San Adrián

Calahorra

Aldeanueva de Ebro

Arnedo

C115

A68

Alfaro

R. Cidacos

C123

Cervera del Rio Alhama

Rioja Alavesa

Rioja Alta

Rioja Baja

Rioja – the Bordeaux Legacy

The Rioja covers some 49,700 hectares (123,000 acres) of vineyards. It is the only wine region of Spain to have been granted the status of *Denominación de Origen Calificada*, equivalent to the Italian D.O.C.G. To achieve this status, a region must demonstate over a long period that it can consistently produce wine of the very highest quality.

Harvesting Tempranillo grapes in the Rioja Alta.

IMPERIAL
RESERVA
1978
Rioja

Compañía Vinícola del Norte de España, s.a.

13% Vol.   HARO LA RIOJA
75 cl. e

PRODUCE OF SPAIN

It often comes as a surprise to discover the extent of the Rioja's debt to Bordeaux. For it is this great French region that has been chiefly responsible, however indirectly, for the two boom periods that created the Riojan industry as it exists today.

Up to the middle of the last century, the Rioja made wine in a similar way to other Spanish regions, crushing the grapes and fermenting their juice in open stone *lagares*.

Then, in the 1860s, the phylloxera, a louse that attacks the vine and destroys its roots, laid waste the vineyards of France, forcing the wine brokers or *négociants* to seek other sources of supply. In the Rioja they found a region with enormous potential, opened up buying offices and brought with them their technicians and wine-makers.

Oak vats and barrels

The phylloxera eventually spread to Spain but by then the Rioja had grown and many of the methods of ageing and production introduced by the French had taken firm root.

Bordeaux's greatest legacy was the use of oak. The wines were fermented in huge oak vats and, after a period of rest, were pumped into the classic Bordelais barrel of 222 litres (roughly 50 gallons) where they were aged for several years. It is this period of oak ageing that is chiefly responsible for the distinctive character of traditional Riojas. The whites deepen to an almost golden colour and achieve a unique concentration of fruit, flavour and acidity. The reds, on the other hand, lighten to a dark tawny colour with a wonderful balance between fruit and oakiness. All have the distinctive soft vanilla flavour that is the region's hallmark.

The boom of the 1970s

Not all the region's wines are made in this way, however. For, in the 1970s, the Rioja experienced another revolution that was as far reaching as the one of the 19th century. Again Bordeaux acted as a catalyst.

In the first years of the decade, claret prices exploded and wine traders once more had to look to other regions. They soon re-discovered the Rioja, where wine was still being made in the way it had been in Bordeaux before the phylloxera. From relative obscurity, the region was dragged into the international limelight. Demand triggered off an immense flow of investment. It also brought in new personnel, wine-makers and marketing experts who knew what

was drunk and how wine was made in other countries. Their influence was quickly felt.

The new wines

The greatest change introduced was in the production of whites and rosés. The 'modernists' began to ferment them at low temperatures to preserve their aroma and freshness. They also began to release the wines younger.

The change in the red wines was more subtle. Instead of ageing them for long periods in barrel, bottling and releasing them six months later, they began to age the wines for less time in the barrel and for longer in bottle. The result is that they are less oaky but perhaps more complex and elegant.

The original oak fermentation vats at Marqués de Riscal installed by the French technician Jean Pineau (see pages 35-6).

The Tempranillo is the leading grape variety of the region, covering some 52 per cent of the entire vineyard area. It is followed by the Garnacha which covers about 22 per cent and lesser quantities of Graciano and Mazuelo, usually planted in small parcels in the Alta.

White wines are usually made from the Viura but the Malvasía and the Garnacha Blanca are also permitted.

29

Wine Country of the Rioja Baja

The tree-lined central square in the old Roman city of Calahorra in the Rioja Baja is famous for a notorious casino where, in the past, whole estates are said to have been gambled away.

ALFARO

RECOMMENDED HOTEL
Hotel Palacios Ctra. Zaragoza 6. Tel: 18 01 00. Fax: 18 36 22. Ask here to visit Bodega Palacio Remondo next door.

RECOMMENDED RESTAURANT
Asador San Roque San Roque 3. Tel: 18 28 88. Regional Riojan food.

CALAHORRA

RECOMMENDED RESTAURANTS
Casa Mateo Pl. Quintiliano 15. Tel: 13 00 09.
La Taverna de la Cuarta Esquina Cuatro Esquinas 16. Tel: 13 43 55.
Both have very good food at reasonable prices.

Following the suggested route (see page 26), the tour begins in the Rioja Baja, the warmest and lowest of the region's three sub-zones, a flat plain of ochre-coloured fields lying alongside the great Ebro river. As few bodegas are based here, it is not an area often visited by wine buffs. But there are quiet, pleasant towns, several good restaurants serving local produce and a few small but upcoming wine companies.

The Garnacha is the dominant grape variety here and produces wines with good colour, body and a comparatively high level of alcohol.

Alfaro
From Cintruénigo, where the tour of Navarra ended, it is a small step across the regional border to Alfaro. This is a small agricultural town and its main feature is the Hotel Palacios. As it also has a wine and fossil museum, an excellent restaurant and is next to Bodegas Palacio Remondo, it is a good overnight stop. Nearby there is also one of the best restaurants of the Rioja Baja, the Asador San Roque which offers good regional food with excellent vegetable dishes.

Calahorra
Alternatively continue along the N232 to the pleasant old Roman city of Calahorra. With its notorious casino, where whole estates are said to have been gambled away, this is

one of the largest towns of the Rioja, a busy commercial centre serving the local agricultural community. The town has several good restaurants and one of the region's two Paradors.

Quel and Grávalos

Calahorra is not a wine town, however. If it is bodegas you are after, then drive south to Arnedo. From there the narrow C115 will take you along the Cidacos river to the small town of Quel, home of Bodegas Ontañon.

Otherwise follow the C123 to Grávalos, where you can visit the small, family-owned Bodegas Escudero. These are two of the most exciting wineries in the Rioja Baja and the latter even produces a sparkling wine made from Chardonnay grown in its own vineyards.

Ask for directions at either bodega to the nearby site where dinosaur footprints have been found. Then return to Arnedo for lunch and follow the riverside C115 westwards.

Just before Arnedillo you come to the Molino del Cidacos, a small hotel, restaurant and winery, all housed in an old converted windmill.

The road to Logroño

From Calahorra it is about 50km (30 miles) to Logroño either along the N232 *nacional* or the more expensive A68 *autopista*.

Both of these roads go through the heart of the region to Haro and the Basque country beyond. But the N232 is very busy, with heavy trucks grinding their way north, while the A68 carries very little traffic and is an easy drive, with an exit immediately south of Logroño.

The Rioja Baja is the warmest, driest and flattest of the three Rioja wine sub-zones. The Garnacha grape thrives here, producing fruity wines that are comparatively high in alcohol.

QUEL

Bodegas Ontañon Camino del Molino s/n. Tel: 39 23 49. Fax: 39 21 85. (Lucia Arechavaleta Fernandez). Open every day 1100-1400, 1600-200. Closed Aug. Collection of sculptures and paintings. E.F.TF.WS. ☎

GRAVALOS

Bodegas Escudero Ctra.de Arnedo s/n, 26587 Grávalos. Tel: 39 80 08. Fax: 39 80 70. (Angeles Escudero). Mon-Sat 0900-2000. E.F.TF.WS. ☎ groups of over 20 people only.

ARNEDILLO

RECOMMENDED HOTEL/ RESTAURANT
El Molino de Cidacos Ctra. de Arnedo Km.63.5. Tel: 39 40 63. Good wine shop attached.

Logroño

LOGRONO

Bodegas Marqués de Murrieta Finca YGAY, Ctra. Logroño-Zaragoza Km.5, Logroño. Tel: 25 81 00. Fax: 25 16 06. (Alfonso Troya). Open every day 1200-1400. Closed Dec, Aug, Easter. Wine museum. No groups of more than 10. WS. ☎

Bodegas Olarra S.A. Polígono de Cantabria s/n, 26006 Logroño. Tel: 23 52 99. Fax: 25 37 03. (Alvaro Castrejana). Mon-Fri 0900-1300, 1500-1900. Sat mornings by request. Closed Aug. Wine and wine accessories shop. E.TF.WS. ☎

Despite its great prosperity, Logroño is a relatively quiet provincial city. It can be busy enough though, particularly on Saturday nights when the student population throngs the tapas bars (for explanation see page 100) of the Calle de los Laureles near the central square, and in general the bars and restaurants are overflowing. But the ostentatious display of wealth which you find in Spain's other rich cities is missing. The Riojano is certainly no miser and he likes to eat and drink, but, perhaps because he is still essentially a countryman, he keeps his money safely in the bank.

Logroño is a real wine city. Famous labels stare out at you from bottles in the windows of grocery and wine shops, while the wine lists of its restaurants seem to burst with local pride, displaying what almost amounts to a roll of honour of the Spanish wine industry.

The old bodegas...

The city is also the home of several leading bodegas. Some 3km (2 miles) from the city centre, on the south-bound N232, is the famous Bodegas

Marqués de Murrieta. Founded in 1848, it claims to be the oldest existing wine company in the Rioja, and is now owned by a count from Galicia who has continued the firm's aristocratic lineage. The entrance to the winery is tricky, as it can only be approached from the southbound *nacional* and is badly signposted. But, for lovers of wine history, a visit, which has to be arranged in advance, is a must.

Closer to the city centre, on the western bank of the river, is another historic company, Bodegas Franco-Españolas, founded in 1901 by a Frenchman fleeing from phylloxera. Again, the whole complex, with its extensive underground cellars, is lovingly maintained.

...and the new
Another must is Bodegas Olarra. Built during the boom of the 1970s by a steel magnate, it represents the modern face of the Rioja and is located in an industrial estate on the outskirts of the city. It is, however, a splendid building, modelled on the wineries of California, and built in the shape of a Y to represent the three sub-zones of the region. It produces a wide range of wine styles, including a sparkler, all of which are offered in the bodega shop which also has wine accessories and souvenirs.

Yet another worthwhile visit is to the family-owned Bodegas Martínez Bujanda in the tiny hamlet of Oyón just a few kilometres to the north of the city. Again, this is a modern, high-tech winery, but it produces a superb range of wines and is one of the most respected wine companies in the region.

Finally enjoy Logroño as the locals do. Go out for tapas on the Calle de los Laureles, followed by dinner at one of the recommended restaurants.

LOGRONO (cont.)

RECOMMENDED WINE SHOP
La Catedral del Vino
Clle. Portales 25.

RECOMMENDED RESTAURANTS
Cachetero Laurel 3. Tel: 22 84 63. The city's best. Very good food. Expensive.
Las Cubanas San Agustín 17. Tel: 22 00 50. Good Riojan cuisine.
Iruña Laurel 8. Tel: 22 00 64. Good Riojan cuisine.

OYON
Bodegas Martínez Bujanda
Camino Viejo s/n, 01320 Oyón. Tel: 12 21 88. Fax: 12 21 11. (Carlos Martínez Bujanda). Mon-Fri 0830-1230, 1500-1700. Closed Aug. E.F.G.I.WS. ☎

Bodegas Franco-Españolas in Logroño represents Rioja's union of French and Spanish wine-making traditions.

Rioja Alta and Alavesa

NAVARRETE
Bodegas Corral Ctra. de Logroño Km.10, 26370 Navarrete. Tel: 44 01 93. Fax: 44 01 95. (Andrea Stehle). Mon-Fri 1000-1300, 1500-1900. Sat 1000-1400. Closed Aug. E.G.F.WS. ☎

LAGUARDIA
Bodegas Palacio San Lazaro 1, 01300 Laguardia. Tel: 10 01 51. Fax: 10 02 97. (Begoña Viniegra, Natividad Coca). Tue-Sun 1200-1400. E.TF.WS. (☎ groups only). To book rooms at the attached hotel write/fax to the same address.

Vineyards line the banks of the river Oja in the Rioja Alta. Here the vines are trained along wires, an unusual sight in Spain, where they are mainly grown as bushes.

If the N232 *nacional* is busy to the east of Logroño, it is even more so to the west. Unfortunately, unless you want to go straight to Haro and miss out on the towns in between, there is no good alternative, as continually joining and leaving the A68 *autopista* is very complicated.

Furthermore, the N232 is undoubtedly the best way to see the countryside of the Rioja Alta and Alavesa, with glimpses of vineyards and good views of the river and the Sierra beyond. Once you get off the *nacionales* on to the small C roads, there is relatively little traffic, but the road surfaces often leave a lot to be desired.

Fuenmayor
The N232 leaves Logroño from the south-west and it is no more than 20 to 30 minutes to Fuenmayor, the first of the Alta's wine towns.

The centre of the town is dominated by the church and the Casa Real, a crumbling stately home, and all around the central square are bars which, at the start of the harvest, the *vendimia*, are packed with itinerant workers waiting for the picking to begin. As in Logroño, Saturday night suddenly transforms the town, even in the winter, when these bars fill up with cheerful grape farmers and wine-makers coming into town for a glass of wine or two.

Navarrete
From Fuenmayor it is a short skip across the A68 to Bodegas Corral in Navarrete. This is a respected wine producer founded in 1974 and housed in a winery built following the traditional style of architecture of the region. From Navarrete the N120 will take you to Najera with its beautiful monastery of Santa Maria la Real.

Alternatively, from Fuenmayor head northwards across the Ebro into the Rioja Alavesa in the direction of Laguardia.

The Alavesa

Here, despite still being in the delimited zone of the Rioja, you enter the Basque country and the province of Alava. This is the heart of the Rioja Alavesa, where the Tempranillo grape is king and, to the discerning palate, the wines produced are different, warmer, richer and more luscious than the more austere and elegant wines of the Alta.

In Laguardia, standing against the backdrop of the Sierra Cantabria, is Bodegas Palacio, which has recently opened a small hotel in the old 19th century bodegas. This makes it an ideal place to stay, and the hotel will organise a wide range of activities such as hiking, bicycle touring and cross-country horseback riding.

Bodega visits

Laguardia can also be used as a base for visits to two interesting bodegas in the vicinity. The first is to Viñedos del Contino, a small château-style estate in Laserna owned by C.V.N.E. of Haro (see page 39).

The second is to La Granja Nuestra Señora de Remelluri, which is further up into the mountains. This is another quality-conscious firm, and the winery is a contrast between the latest wine-making equipment and the ancient winery buildings, which were once a farm run by the Cistercian monastery of Nuestra Señora de Toloño. The property has a small hermitage, a wine museum and some tombs of archeological interest. Ask at the hotel for directions.

Wine is still bottled by hand at the López de Heredia winery in Haro (see also page 39). This company remains loyal to traditional wine-making skills.

Elciego and Marqués de Riscal

From Laguardia, another small road leads down from the Sierra to the lovely town of Elciego.

For the wine historian, this is a place of pilgrimage, as it contains the famous and historic winery of Marqués de Riscal. This was the first winery in the region to be built along French lines by the technician Jean Pineau in 1868.

Just to show how close the Rioja came to missing its modern fame and reputation, it is worth briefly recounting the story of this influential Frenchman.

LAGUARDIA (cont.)
La Granja Nuestra
Señora de Remelluri
Ctra. Rivas de Tereso s/n, Laguardia. Tel: 33 12 74. Fax: 33 14 41. (Telmo Rodriguez). Mon-Sat 1100-1400. Closed Aug. Museum, hermitage. E.TF.WS. ☎

RECOMMENDED RESTAURANT
Marixa Sancho Abarca 8. Tel: 10 01 65. Good regional food.

LASERNA
Viñedos del Contino
Finca San Gregorio, 01309 Laserna. Tel: 10 02 01. Fax: 12 11 14. (Juan Antonio Bonilla). Mon-Fri 0900-1300, 1530-1800. Closed Aug. WS. ☎

The historic bodega of Marqués de Riscal in Elciego was the birthplace of the modern Riojan wine industry.

ELCIEGO
Vinos de los Herederos del Marqués de Riscal
Clle. Torrea 1, 01340
Elciego. Tel: 10 60 00. Fax:
10 60 23. (Ruth Sutton).
Mon-Fri 0800-1300, 1430-
1730. Closed Aug.
E.TF.WS.☎

CENICERO
Bodegas Riojanas
Estación 1-21, Cenicero.
Tel: 45 40 50. Fax:
45 45 29. (Felipe Nadal
Frias). Mon-Fri 1130.
E.TF.WS. ☎
Unión-Viti-Vinícola,
Bodegas Marqués de
Cáceres Ctra. de Logroño
s/n, 26350 Cenicero. Tel:
45 50 64. Fax: 45 44 00.
(Anne Vallejo). Mon-Fri
0900-1330, 1500-1600.
Closed Aug and first week
in Sep. E.F.WS. ☎

Jean Pineau and Riscal

Pineau was originally employed by the authorities of Alava to advise the province's grape farmers and small wine-makers. The measures he suggested were expensive, particularly the ageing of wine in oak barrels and the replanting of vineyards with French grape varieties, and were beyond the means of the region's small producers.

It was just as his bags were packed to go home that Pineau was approached by Camilo Hurtado de Amézaga, the Marqués de Riscal, and commissioned to design a winery, using those of Bordeaux as a model. Many of his innovations are now outdated, but the winery, built of soft sandstone and standing in the middle of its vineyards, still stands as a testimony to the French contribution to the Riojan wine industry.

Cenicero

From Elciego it is a 15-minute drive along a bumpy but scenic road to Cenicero on the N232. Here we are back in the Rioja Alta, and Cenicero is a real wine town. One in every three hectares here are planted with vines and, in good years, the town and its two neighbours – Huércanos and Uruñuela – produce more than 21 million litres (about five million gallons) of high-quality wine.

It is a congenial place, too. Every year during the first week of September the town embarks on ten days of uninterrupted eating, drinking and playing to celebrate its patron saint, Santa Daría. On the final day there is the ritual pressing of the first wine of the year.

It is great fun. But some of the bodegas, of which the town has many, shut down for the duration, so avoid this week if winery visits are your main concern.

Cenicero's bodegas

There are many co-operatives and bodegas in the vicinity but the two most interesting are in the town itself.

Bodegas Riojanas stands on the town's main road near the railway line and was in built in 1890 by French technicians. What appeals about this company is its combination of the old and the new. Stainless steel tanks rise alongside old oak vats and the modern bottling line lies beside rows of oak barrels. And the firm produces excellent wines that are representative of the region as a whole.

Bodegas Marqués de Cáceres

Just around the corner on the eastern approach to the town is the last but in many ways the most important of Cenicero's bodegas, Marqués de Cáceres. Here we find more recent French influence as the firm is partly owned and run by the charming Franco-Spanish Forner family who also own Château Camensac in Bordeaux.

When the company was founded in the early 1970s, it soon became one of the region's great innovators, introducing methods of ageing and production that were in current use in Bordeaux, such as a short period of oak ageing for the reds and the fermentation and release of whites and rosés with no ageing at all. Regarded as revolutionary at the time, these methods have now been imitated by many companies.

The lovely town of Elciego, one of the main wine centres of the Rioja Alavesa, is the home of several bodegas, including that of Marqués de Riscal.

Ollauri and Haro

HARO

Federico Paternina S.A.
Av. Santo Domingo 11, Haro.
Tel: 31 05 50. Fax: 31 27 78.
(Jesus Villanueva, Alex
Candina). Mon-Fri 0900-
1300, 1500-1700. Closed Aug
and Sep. TF.WS. ☎
Also apply to this address for
visits to the cellars in Ollauri.

Bodegas Muga Barrio de la
Estación s/n, 26200 Haro.
Tel: 31 18 25. Fax: 31 28 67.
Mon-Fri 1100-1600. Closed
last week June. E.F.TF.WS.

**R. López de Heredia
Viña Tondonia S.A.** Av.
de Vizcaya 3, 26200 Haro.
Tel: 31 01 27. Fax:
41 02 44. (Julián José Osses
Santos, Maria José López de
Heredia). In winter Mon-Fri
0830-1300, 1500-1830. In
summer 0800-1400. Closed
last week June, 15 Aug-15
Sep. E.F.TF.WS. ☎

**Compañía Vinícola del
Norte de España (C.V.N.E.)**
Av. Costa del Vino 21,
26200 Haro. Tel: 31 06 50.
Fax: 31 28 19. (Lorenzo
Carro). Mon-Fri 0900-1300.
Closed Aug, last week June,
second week Sep. TF.WS. ☎

La Rioja Alta S.A. Av.
Vizcaya s/n, 26200 Haro.
Tel: 31 03 46. Fax: 31 28
54. (Marta Enciso, Nuria
Corcuera). Mon-Fri 0900-
1800. E.TF.WS. A visit to
sister company Torre de
Oña in Laguardia can be
arranged here.

RECOMMENDED WINE SHOP
Mi Bodega Santo Tomas
13. Also has a selection of
regional foods.

RECOMMENDED HOTEL
Los Agustinos San
Agustín 2. Tel: 31 13 08.
Fax: 30 31 48. Housed in a
14th-century convent.

From Cenicero, the N232 continues its steady rise to the town of Haro. Some 2km (over a mile) from the first exit, there is a turn-off to the south that leads to the quiet hamlet of Ollauri. If you can arrange a visit to the Paternina winery, this could be one of the highlights of a tour of the Rioja.

Ollauri and Paternina

Federico Paternina is one of the largest wine companies of the region, with a modern complex on the outskirts of Haro. But its deep, underground cellars at Ollauri, dug by Portuguese workers during the 16th century, are one of the Rioja's great showpieces. There is something almost frightening about them, with their long, low corridors, their blackened, musty, dripping walls and their bins of old bottles.

Federico Paternina takes great pride in its cellars, which were carved out of the rock beneath the hamlet of Ollauri in the 16th century. They are a national monument in the Rioja.

Haro and its bodegas

Travelling on up the road, you come to the buzzing, prosperous town of Haro. This is the centre of the Rioja Alta, and the capital of the Denomination of Origin. Haro has one of the leading enological stations in Spain – with a wine museum attached – and several wine companies and fine restaurants.

If you are approaching from the east, you may be tempted to take the first signposted exit, entering the town through some ugly suburbs and ending up somewhere in the maze of streets around the central square.

However, it is much better to continue on the N232, passing a hotel, to the second exit which leaves the road in a broad arc to the right and then crosses over a bridge. This will lead you straight to the Barrio de La Estación quarter around the railway station, the area with the greatest concentration of bodegas.

Many of these are very prestigious companies with old traditions and varied histories.

First, there is the tastefully modernized but traditional and highly respected La Rioja Alta, which has recently been expanded. Across the road is López de Heredia with its fairytale Swiss tower, a firm that prides itself on its unbroken adherence to traditional methods of production and ageing, and whose winery is virtually a working museum.

The larger, very prestigious Compañía Vinícola del Norte de España (C.V.N.E.) produces a wide range of high quality wines embracing all the different styles produced in the region.

Bodegas Bilbaínas has the most extensive underground cellars in the Rioja, while the charming, rather magical Bodegas Muga has a winery housed in lovely old sandstone buildings, which is almost a monument to the oak barrel and the vat.

A visit to any of these companies, regarded by many as the real aristocrats of the Rioja, will be a rewarding experience. The other, more modern, wineries south of the town tend to pale into insignificance.

The town centre

Haro is also a town worth wandering around, and it is a good place to stay overnight. It has a pleasant central square surrounded by arcades, with old houses dating back to the 18th century. The church of Santo Tomás is older. Accommodation can be found at the historic Los Agostinos hotel (see opposite page), the unpretentious Hostal Iturrimuri on the N232 or the great Parador at Santo Domingo de la Calzada some 15 minutes' drive out of town.

The tower of the López de Heredia winery is one of Haro's most famous landmarks.

Furthermore, the town has some good, traditional restaurants, including the famous Mesón Terete in the centre. Specializing in lamb roasted in a baker's oven, and served at simple wooden tables, it is a must for all travellers in the Rioja.

To continue from the Rioja to the wine regions of Old Castile, the traveller can take the N111 from Logroño and then the N122 after Soria to Aranda de Duero. Or – and this is the suggested route, particularly in the winter – follow the N232 or the A68 northwards and join the A1 or N1 which lead down to the historic city of Burgos. From there the N1 goes straight to Aranda.

HARO (cont.)

RECOMMENDED RESTAURANTS
Mesón Terete Lucrecia Arana 17. Tel: 31 00 11. Traditional Riojan food.
Beethoven I & II Santo Tomás 3-5 and 10. Tel: 31 11 81. Run by the same management. The first is an elegant restaurant, the second a more relaxed *mesón*. Good regional food.

BRINAS

RECOMMENDED WINE SHOP/ RESTAURANT/HOTEL
Portal de la Rioja Ctra. Vitoria-Logroño Km.42. Tel: 31 14 80. Just a short distance from Haro and well worth a visit. Good selection of regional wines, food, arts and crafts.

Food and Festivals of the Rioja

An elaborately framed menu outside Mesón Terete in Haro (see page 39 for details) announces regional dishes such as tender roast lamb.

RIOJAN CUISINE

The excellence of Riojan cuisine is based on the sheer quality of its raw materials. Fresh fish is brought down from the Basque coast and lamb is reared in the hills of the Alta and Alavesa. The Baja is one of the great gardens of Spain, producing excellent vegetables: artichokes, asparagus, tomatoes, lettuce and peppers.

Lamb occupies a central position in the local cuisine. Dishes range from the classic *Cordero asado* to lamb chops grilled over a fire of vine shoots, another regional favourite. The local *chorizo*, not as spicy as in the rest of Spain, adds bite to stews such as *Patatas a la Riojana*.

The arrival of the year's first asparagus is an important date in the region's gastronomic calendar. Peppers, preferably the famous *pimientos del piquillo*, make an appearance in most local meals, either in stews, or baked or fried and served alongside meat, or stuffed with various other ingredients. The greatest vegetable dish, however, is

FOOD SPECIALITIES

Callos a La Riojana Tripe cooked with whole *chorizos*, ham, nuts and several different vegetables and spices.

Chuleta de Ternera a la Riojana This dish is typical of the region as it combines grilled meat, in this case veal chops, sprinkled with chopped garlic and parsley, and peppers.

Menestra de Verduras A great local favourite which combines the region's wonderful vegetables – artichokes, peas and asparagus – together with cured ham and eggs which are either hard boiled or beaten into the mixture.

Cordero asado Lamb baked in an earthenware dish and served with a salad – try the baby lettuce split in half and mixed with vinaigrette, garlic and anchovies.

Patatas a la Riojana A simple and hearty potato stew cooked with *chorizo*, garlic, onion and sometimes a little white wine.

Pimientos rellenos de Codornices Peppers stuffed with quails.

Solomillo al vino de Rioja One of the few great local dishes where wine is used in its preparation. Beef steaks are macerated in red wine and brandy and are cooked with mushrooms and small onions.

the *Menestra de Verduras* which shows off the local produce at its very best.

WINE FESTIVALS

Virtually every town in the Rioja has a patron saint's day which is a public holiday when the bars and streets are full until the early hours of the morning and the *zurracapote* flows. This is a mixture of wine, fruit and cinnamon which is prepared by the small wine-makers of the town and is offered to friends and visitors to drink on the premises.

Apart from Santa Daría in Cenicero, the two main festivals take place in Haro and Logroño.

The first is the famous *Batalla del Vino* on St Peter's Day, 29 June. It starts with a ceremony at the chapel of San Felices, some 3km (2 miles) from Haro. Then the participants, usually dressed in white, return on foot to Haro, literally drenching each other with wine.

By comparison, the *Feria de San Mateo* in Logroño on St Matthew's Day, 21 September, is a rather subdued affair. Traditionally it was supposed to mark the beginning of the *vendimia* but, these days, it is usually well under way by then. This is a serious religious festival, but afterwards there is plenty of jollity – and drinking – in the streets.

The Batalla del Vino *attracts hordes of local people. The participants make their way back to Haro from San Felices, squirting each other with wine from wineskins as they go.*

41

Aragon

Steeped in history, the ancient Kingdom of Aragon lies between Catalonia to the east and the great vineyards of the Rioja Baja and Navarra to the west. It is believed that its wine industry dates back to the 3rd century B.C. when its people drank wine mixed with honey. Today, it has some 70,000 hectares (over 170,000 acres) of vineyard, most of which are planted to the west and south of Zaragoza, the capital.

The region produces mostly red wines, which are usually almost purple in colour with immense body and alcohol, and are high in tannins. In a tradition that goes back to the time of the phylloxera in France, many of these are used for blending. And, as the province is dominated by its co-operatives, it is neither the most dynamic nor advanced of Spain's wine regions. Each of its four Denominations, however, hides its odd gem, and these, combined with the majesty of its flat, ochre-coloured plains to the south and its views over the foothills of the Pyrenees to the north, offer a fair reward to the wine traveller en route from the Rioja or Navarra to Catalonia.

Aragon's harsh climate and rocky landscape tend to preserve the older way of life. Many of the villages of central Aragon have changed little in the past century.

The route outlined below is for drivers entering the region from Navarra or the Rioja Baja, and leads in a zig-zag from west to east. Those entering from Catalonia can follow the route in reverse.

From Cintruénigo where the tour of Navarra ended, drivers are advised to rejoin either the N232 or the A68, follow it to Magallón (about 50km or 30 miles) and continue to Borja.

From Borja, the centre of the Campo de Borja Denomination, the small C220 leads to Cariñena (60km or 37 miles), capital of the largest Denomination.

Then it is up the N330 to Zaragoza where travellers can either enter the city or use the well-signposted ring road system and rejoin the N330, which leads to Huesca (120km or 70 miles altogether). Here one enters the city before branching off on to the N240 to the Denomination of Somontano.

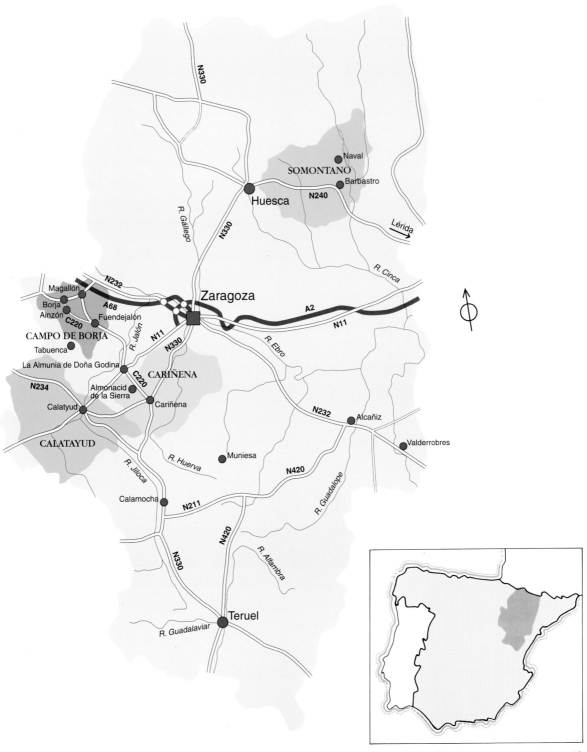

Wines and Wine Villages of Aragon

AINZON
Bodegas Bordejé Ctra. Borja-Rueda Km.3, Ainzón, (Zaragoza). Tel/Fax: 86 80 80. (Fernando and José Ignacio Bordejé). Time and date of visits to be arranged in advance. Open all year. E.F.TF.WS. ☎

CARINENA

RECOMMENDED RESTAURANT
Mesón el Escudo on the C220 on the outskirts of the town. Good, hearty Aragonese cuisine.

HUESCA

RECOMMENDED RESTAURANT
Venta del Sotón Ctra. Tarragona-San Sebastian Km.227. Tel: 27 02 41. Just outside the city, with a huge central fireplace and good regional food.

BARBASTRO
Bodegas Lalanne
Castillo San Marcos, Barbastro, (Huesca). Tel/Fax: 31 06 89. (Nuria Canales). Mon-Fri 0900-1300, 1500-1900. E.F.TF.WS. ☎

RECOMMENDED RESTAURANT
Flor Goya 3. Tel: 31 10 56. *Haute cuisine.*

The 9800 hectares (24,200 acres) of Campo de Borja, the most westerly of Aragon's D.O.s, surround the wine towns of Fuendejalón, Magallón, Borja, Ainzón and Tabuenca. Each town has its big co-operative, with the largest and most advanced at Borja on the Zaragoza-Soria road.

These co-operatives dominate the Denomination's production, making sound reds and rosés which can be pleasant and fruity drinking when young. But they are dark, lugubrious places to visit.

More interesting is Bodegas Bordejé in Ainzón. This is a privately-owned firm housed in old buildings on the outskirts of the town with deep, underground cellars built towards the end of the 18th century. And it makes what is generally regarded as the best Cava of the region as well as some interesting, oak-aged *reservas*.

Cariñena
From Ainzón, take the C220, which leads directly to the town of Cariñena, the centre of the Denomination of the same name. With its inexpensive hotel and a good restaurant on its outskirts serving regional food, this is a convenient town in which to stay overnight.

Cariñena is a real wine town surrounded by nearly 5000 hectares (over 12,000 acres) of vineyard. It is also the home of one of the largest co-operatives of the region, the Bodegas San Valero on the N330 to Teruel. This produces a wide range of wines that are typical of the Denomination. But the sheer size of the operation is indicative of one of the weaknesses of the region. With its production dominated by huge co-operatives, Cariñena has not moved

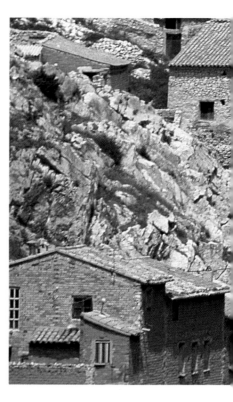

as quickly as other Denominations and the style of its wines is now rather old fashioned.

The wines
As Cariñena and Campo de Borja share the same climate and soil structures, and are dependent on the same grape, their wines are broadly similar. Curiously, the Cariñena grape itself, which is still used in Catalonia, is no longer important in this part of Aragon. The extremes of climate, with baking hot summers and numbing cold winters, have ensured that the hardy Garnacha reigns supreme, producing robust, hard and strong wines that soften with age.

Further north in the province of Huesca, however, the very much smaller Denomination of Somontano produces wines that are quite different in character. Lying in the

foothills of the Pyrenees, it is higher and its soils are lighter. More importantly it has a greater variety of grapes, with noble French varieties such as the Chardonnay, the Cabernet Sauvignon and the Merlot rubbing shoulders with local ones, the excellent Moristel and the more usual Tempranillo, Garnacha, Macabeo and Parellada.

Furthermore, the region has a handful of innovative private companies that are quality minded and their initiative has driven the region forward. Somontano may be a small Denomination, but it produces some excellent wines.

The bodegas of Somontano

The largest of these firms is the Co-operativa de Somontano de Sobrabe on the road to Naval just outside Barbastro. By Spanish standards it is a small co-operative, but it accounts for 90 per cent of the region's production. And, although its winery is not very interesting, it produces top quality wines.

Just a few kilometres down the same road is Bodegas Lalanne. Built in 1847 by a French family, this is a leafy, ramshackle place, more like a Latin American *hacienda* than a winery. But it produces an excellent range of wines, many of them made with French varieties.

Finally, there are two very much smaller, family-owned firms, Bodegas Fábregas in Barbastro and Bodegas Monclus in Radiquero, just up the road from Lalanne. Again, both produce excellent wines.

From Barbastro the N240 leads to Lérida and the turn-off to Raimat (see page 115) is about 10km (6 miles) from the city.

Almonacid de la Sierra is the home of Bodegas López Pelayo.

Old Castile

Known today as Castilla-León, Old Castile was the heartland of Spain in the Middle Ages. It was here that the Christian rulers of the North finally forged a united country through the marriage of Isabella, Queen of Castile, to King Ferdinand of Aragon in 1469 and paved the way to the defeat of Granada, the last Moorish bastion in the Iberian peninsula. And it was here that the united Spaniards established their political and religious centre, the foundation for one of history's greatest empires. This is a region rich in history that offers the tourist a great deal – mighty castles, medieval cities and innumerable churches and monasteries. Its simple and hearty cuisine is justly famous and its wines are increasingly being regarded in Spain as among the very best in the country.

It must be remembered, however, that Old Castile lies on the *meseta*, the highest plateau in Europe. Most of it is over 600 metres (2000ft) above sea level, and the climate is extreme, with temperatures rising to 40°C in the summer and plunging to minus 20°C in the winter. It is best, therefore, to make this trip in spring or autumn, when conditions will be at their best.

The route to Old Castile

From Haro where the tour of the Rioja ended, there is a journey north of 10km (6 miles) before you reach the beginning of the A1 *autopista*, which heads down to Burgos, the first great city of Old Castile. The toll-free N1 runs almost parallel.

The Ribera del Duero

From Burgos the N1 leads straight to Aranda de Duero, 75km (47 miles) away, which is the starting point of the route through the Ribera del Duero. From Aranda take the C619 in the direction of Palencia to the towns of La Horra and Sotillo de la Ribera nearby. Other side roads lead to Roa, Pedrosa and Peñafiel.

Toro and Rueda

Tordesillas, 25km (16 miles) south of Valladolid, is a convenient base for trips to Toro and Rueda, the capitals of their Denominations. Thereafter, the road heads for Madrid.

For those with little time to spare, the NVI leads south to the town of Adanero, where it is possible to join the A6. Both roads then cross the Sierra de Guadarrama to Madrid. During the winter, and particularly in snow, the *autopista* is recommended.

Segovia

For those with more time, one or two days spent exploring the mountain villages of Segovia can be very rewarding. From Medina del Campo, the small C112 leads eastwards to the towns of Sepúlveda, Riaza and Pedraza. The N110 then leads back to Segovia. From there, the N603 joins the A6 or the NVI which takes you across the Sierra to Madrid.

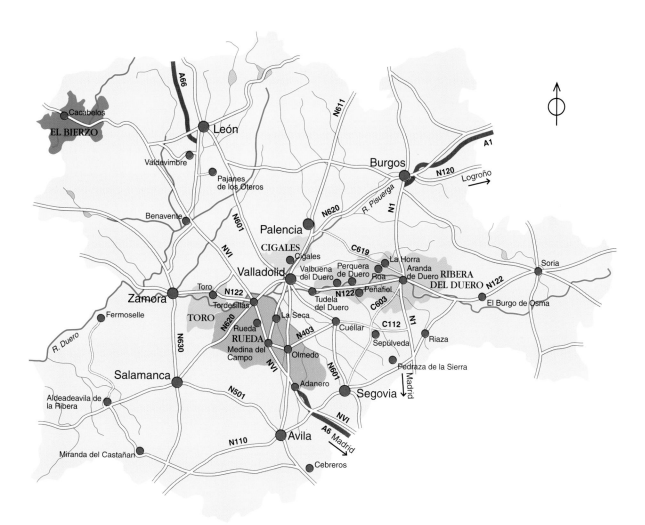

The Wines of Old Castile

Ribera del Duero

Granted its status as a Denomination in 1983, the Ribera del Duero's wine-growing area is expanding and has now reached over 10,000 hectares (about 25,000 acres).

The vineyards follow the river valley, but most are concentrated in the area of Aranda de Duero. The Tinto Fino grape (also known as the Tinto del País, a variant of the Tempranillo) holds pride of place in the region, though it is sometimes blended with other authorized varieties such as the Garnacha and the Albillo.

Toro

Toro has only been delimited since 1987 and embraces vineyards in the provinces of Valladolid and Zamora. The principal grape variety is the red Tinta de Toro which covers some 40 per cent of the vineyard area. The red Tinto Madrid (also known as the Negral) is also authorized, as is the Malvasía used in the production of the region's white wines.

The Denomination covers about 3000 hectares (about 7500 acres).

Rueda

The Denomination of Rueda covers about 6650 hectares (16,500 acres) in the provinces of Segovia, Valladolid and Avila. Although there are still substantial plantings of Palomino, the Verdejo has now taken over as the region's top grape variety with over 50 per cent of the vineyard area.

There are two types of table wines, Rueda, and Rueda Superior, and two *generosos*, Pálido and Dorado Rueda. A small amount of Rueda Espumoso (sparkling wine) is also made.

A woman wheels her barrow through the old town of Peñafiel.

The wine industry of Old Castile dates back to the Visigothic period. By the 13th century its wines were quenching the thirst of the countless pilgrims who made their way to Santiago de Compostela, and the region reached a peak of prosperity when the Catholic monarchs transferred the court to Valladolid. The ancient town of Medina del Campo boasted some 470 wine merchants, and Columbus is said to have taken casks of Toro on his first great voyage of discovery.

When the court moved to Madrid, Old Castile lost its pre-eminence, but its wine industry continued to prosper, selling to the vineless provinces of northern Spain.

The vineyards' retreat

During the past century the region has suffered two major disasters. First, at the turn of the century, came phylloxera, devastating the region's vineyards. Then, at the end of the Civil War in the late 1930s, new Wheat Laws were passed to encourage more wheat production. As a result, Old Castile became Spain's 'bread basket' and the vineyards were neglected.

The variety of wines

The region still produces an immense amount of wine, however, in many different styles: there are, for example, the light and subtle wines of El Bierzo; the famous *claretes* of Cigales, to the north of Valladolid; and the strongly *pétillant* 'needle wines' or *vinos de aguja* of León. More importantly, it has three leading Denominations of Origin: Rueda, Toro, and the Ribera del Duero.

These are small regions that lay in comparative obscurity for many years. But they have recently woken up again and they are now regarded as some of the best in the country.

The Ribera

The largest of these Denominations is the Ribera del Duero which lies on the river Duero to the east of Valladolid. Until recently it was best known abroad for Vega Sicilia, perhaps the most celebrated and certainly the most expensive of Spanish red wines. Highly perfumed and with a wonderful balance between concentrated, fragrant fruit, and an oakiness acquired after long periods of barrel ageing, these wines have always enjoyed immense prestige in Spain. But other, less famous firms producing different but high quality wines are now coming to the fore. And there are many who believe that the denomination has now overtaken the Rioja as Spain's foremost red wine producing region.

Many of the wines are made exclusively from the Tinto Fino grape (see blue data panel, left), but this is

sometimes blended with the other Spanish varieties, the Garnacha and the Albillo (a white variety often used in the production of *claretes*). The influence of Vega Sicilia, however, also resulted in the authorization of the Merlot, Cabernet Sauvignon and Malbec. These are used in small quantities and even at Vega they only account for about 35 per cent of the *coupage*. But they give the wines that extra finesse.

Toro

Toro lies further to the west in the province of Zamora and its wines are very different: thick with tannin and extract, bursting with fruit and with a high level of alcohol. A very special, perhaps an acquired taste.

Rueda

Finally, there is Rueda, a region famous for its fortified wines. Aged in carboy (a huge rounded glass bottle), or transferred from barrel to barrel to produce wines of a uniform character and quality, they recall the wines of Jerez and Montilla. Since the opening of Marqués de Riscal's winery in 1972, however, production of crisp, delicate and fruity white table wines aimed at international markets has increased significantly.

Nevertheless, the story of Old Castile is as yet one of unfulfilled potential. It is producing some outstanding wines and there has been enormous investment in the region's viti- and vinicultural base. But the quantities of wine produced are still comparatively small.

The church of San Pablo in Peñafiel dates back to Romanesque times.

49

The Ribera del Duero

The Ribera del Duero stretches along the banks of the mighty river Duero from El Burgo de Osma to Tudela del Duero. It is the highest of Old Castile's leading Denominations, and just nudges the altitude limit for grape-growing, so its vines are planted on the protected slopes of the fertile river valley.

The valley, with its mists and pine trees, has a special microclimate which is one of the reasons for the exceptional quality of its wines. The other is the grapes. More and more vineyards are being planted with the French varieties but the Tinto Fino remains the region's mainstay. And, when blended with a little Albillo, it produces wines with a fine balance, delicate fruit and intense aromas. Oak ageing makes them smoother and more rounded.

The wine villages

We begin our day in the Ribera by taking the C619 in the direction of Palencia to the small town of La Hora and the family-owned Bodegas Balbás, one of the best in the region. Nearby is the town of Sotillo de la Ribera, home to another very good, family-owned company, Bodegas Ismael Arroyo. More small roads lead on to the modern but very charming and hospitable Bodegas Pérez Pascuas in Pedrosa de Duero. Then cross the river Duero to the town of Peñafiel.

Peñafiel

Dominated by its medieval fortress, Peñafiel is one of the largest towns of the region and is a good place to stop for lunch. Try the Asador Mauro which serves excellent meat cooked in a baker's oven and has a good selection of the local wines. The castle itself, with its spectacular views,

is well worth a visit and houses a wine museum. And do not miss the Plaza del Coso which is ringed with balconied houses from which the inhabitants watch bullfights in the square below. If you have time, take a stroll around the *judería* district.

Winery visits

In the afternoon there are two more interesting wineries to visit. The first

is the local co-operative or Bodegas Protos on the main road with its deep cellars under the castle rock. The second is the Pago de Carraovejas just off the main road to the east of the town. This is a modern winery set in its own vineyards on a slope that faces the castle. And its wines prove just how much potential this region has. Look out also for the wines of Vega Sicilia and Bodegas Alejandro

Deep under Peñafiel's medieval castle the local wine co-operative has excavated cellars from the rock to house its traditional wines.

Fernández. Both these bodegas are closed to the public but their wines, which are very different in style, are often considered as the region's best. Make sure, however, that you buy them only in a good restaurant where they will have been well stored.

PENAFIEL (cont.)
Pago de Carraovejas
Camino de Carraovejas s/n, Peñafiel, (Valladolid). Tel: 48 40 08. Fax: 48 40 28. (Tomás Postigo). Mon-Fri 0900-1300, 1600-1800. E.F.TF.WS. ☎

RECOMMENDED RESTAURANT
Asador Mauro
Atarazanas s/n. Tel: 87 30 14. Roasted meats.

Valladolid, Tordesillas and Toro

A view from Toro towards the river Duero. To the south of the town are the vineyards of the Tierra del Vino *(the Land of Wine). To the north, the great wheatfields of Spain begin to roll, an area known as the* Tierra del Pan *(the Land of Bread).*

From Peñafiel the N122 leads straight to Valladolid. As the former capital of Castile and León in the late Middle Ages, Valladolid has some splendid historic sites. There is the College of San Gregorio, the great 16th-century cathedral, and the house of the great Cervantes, author of Spain's classic *Don Quijote (Quixote)*.

For devotees of food and wine there is the Mesón La Fragua, regarded as the best restaurant of the region. But Valladolid is not a good place for the driver: it is a medieval city, a maze of narrow streets, and its one-way systems make driving around and trying to park a nightmare.

Tordesillas

An alternative is to stay at Tordesillas which is 35km (22 miles) away on the N620. This is another historic little town built on a hill, and it was here that Spain and Portugal divided the New World between them in 1494.

The Convent of Santa Clara, where Joanna the Mad (died 1555), imprisoned by her son the Emperor Charles V, spent the last 40 years of her life, justifies a visit. There is also a very fine Parador Nacional with a good restaurant on the N122, on the outskirts of the town.

The town of Toro

From Tordesillas the town of Toro is 40km (25 miles) along the N122. It is an interesting place with old buildings and an arcaded central square lined with shops and small bars.

Toro also has a very reasonable hotel, the Juan II, which is in the centre of the town and has glorious views over the Vega (plain) del Duero, the river valley, and the vineyards to the south. And Toro's bullring, dating back to 1828, is one of the oldest in the country.

Toro is a small Denomination and has only a handful of wine firms. The most important is Bodegas Fariña whose headquarters and old cellars are in the small town of Casaseca de las Chanas nearby. In Toro itself, however, it has built a brand new, purpose-built winery for its bottling and vinification and a visit to it is an ideal way to taste what are, perhaps, the best wines of the region. A day trip from Tordesillas, therefore, should be a rewarding experience.

Modern developments in Toro

Toro has always been famous in Spain for its big red wines (see page 49). Traditionally, these were almost black in colour, packed with tannin and extract, fruity and very alcoholic.

However, things have changed. The grape-growers are now encouraged to pick earlier to reduce the alcohol levels in the wine, and the period in which the skins are left in contact with the must has been reduced, to make the wines a little lighter. Stainless steel is now installed for cold fermentation and the classic 225-litre (50 U.K./60 U.S. gallons) oak barrel is slowly replacing the massive cherry and chestnut barrels of the past.

The red wines are certainly improving and are becoming more accessible and elegant, while maintaining their great character. The whites, made from Malvasía, are also worth trying.

The façade of San Pablo is one of a number of architectural masterpieces in Valladolid, including the cathedral and one of Spain's oldest universities.

Rueda

Rueda, Old Castile's great white wine-producing Denomination, lies to the south of Valladolid. The capital of the Denomination, the town of Rueda itself, is an easy 10km (6 mile) drive from Tordesillas. It is a dusty, unexciting place, but the line of wine shops along the main street underline its commitment to wine production.

VALLADOLID

RECOMMENDED RESTAURANTS
Mesón La Fragua Paseo de Zorrilla 10. Tel: 33 87 85. High quality Castilian cuisine.
Parrilla de San Lorenzo Pedro Niño 1. Tel: 33 50 88. Housed in part of the Real Monasterio of San Bernando.
Portobello Marina Escobár 5. Tel: 30 95 31. Excellent bar and fish dishes.
El Figón de Recoletos Acera de Recoletos 3. Tel: 39 60 43.

Rueda

Rueda is fortunate to have survived the phylloxera. In the province of Valladolid alone some 55,000 hectares (136,000 acres) of vineyard were lost, and many were never replanted.

Rueda's *generosos*

The phylloxera had another long-lasting effect: because of its higher productivity, the Palomino grape began to replace the Verdejo and became the most widely planted variety. In addition, the whole emphasis of production was switched from table wines to *generosos* (fortified wines) or wines aged in barrel or glass carboy (huge rounded bottle) and bearing a vague similarity to the wines of Jerez and Montilla.

Each of the D.O. Rueda's wines displays the 8-spoked cartwheel symbol. Rueda is made from 25 per cent Verdejo grapes, and varies in alcohol from 11 to 14 per cent.

The small town of Rueda is now the capital of one of Spain's leading white wine Denominations.

The *Dorado* and the *Pálido*

These *generosos* come in two styles: the Dorado Rueda has an alcoholic strength of 14 per cent, and is aged for a minimum of four years, two of which must be in oak barrel, the *crianza*. It relies on the region's traditional grapes, the Verdejo and the Palomino, for its colour.

The Pálido Rueda is the strongest of the *generosos*. It has an alcoholic strength of 15 per cent and is aged also for a minimum of four years, but three of these must be in oak. The style recalls the *generosos* of Montilla and Jerez.

Rueda's table wines

In the 1970s, however, Rueda changed direction. At the beginning of the decade the famous Riojan house of Marqués de Riscal startled the Spanish wine industry by announcing that it was transferring its white wine production to Rueda.

Rueda Superior is made with a minimum of 60 per cent Verdejo or Sauvignon Blanc (though most have more than that). Like Rueda, it varies from 11 to 14 per cent alcohol.

The reason was simple: it was felt that the Verdejo, which is native to the region, was better than the Viura and was capable of producing whites of sufficient quality to put alongside its reds and rosés from the Rioja.

Riscal's purpose-built, space-age style winery on the northern outskirts of the town is impressive. The Verdejo is a delicate variety, and the latest grape crushers were installed, working very gently on the grapes. Stainless steel tanks were also introduced, for cold fermentation, which preserves fruit and aroma.

The results were a revelation: wines of great fragrance, with lovely, delicate fruit and a refreshing edge of acidity. Nor did Riscal stop there. It also began to make wines with the Sauvignon Blanc which it grew in its own vineyards on an experimental basis. This variety has now been authorized and produces wines of equal quality.

Other bodegas

Encouraged by Riscal's success, other local firms have begun investing and have looked again at their table wines. The most important of these is Vinos Sanz at the southern limit of the town. Its winery is a bit ramshackle but it produces some good wines, the best of which are bottled under the Sanz label. It also produces a red made from locally-planted Tempranillo.

Also try the region's excellent sparkling wines, which contain a minimum of 85 per cent of the Verdejo grape.

Queen Isabella, one of Spain's most famous monarchs, was a frequent visitor here at the mighty castle of La Mota in Medina del Campo (see page 56).

RUEDA
Vinos Blancos de Castilla Ctra. La Coruña Km.172,600, 47490 Rueda, (Valladolid). Tel: 86 90 29. Fax: 86 85 63. (Raquel Herrero). Mon-Fri 0900-1300, 1500-1900. Closed Aug. E.TF.WS. ☎
Vinos Sanz Ctra. Madrid-La Coruña Km.170.5, 47490 Rueda, (Valladolid). Tel: 86 81 00. Fax: 86 81 17. (Juan Carlos Ayala). Mon-Fri 0900-1800. Closed Aug. F.TF.WS. ☎

RECOMMENDED BARS
Try the **Leonés** and the **Arenal** on the main road going through the town.

The Mountains of Segovia

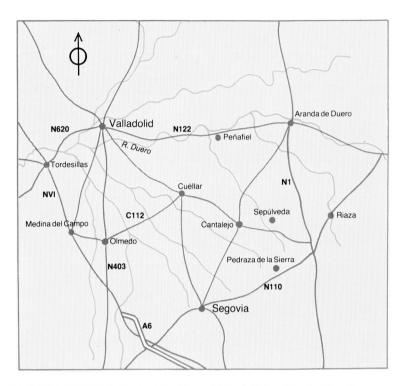

Then take the small C112 that leads east from Medina towards Sepúlveda.

The *hornos de asar*

Old Castile has always been famous for its roasting ovens or *hornos de asar*. Heated with fires of pine wood, vine shoots or eucalyptus, these are made with bricks or mud in a conical shape and are used to bake bread or roast meat. The results are magnificent: large, round, golden loaves or succulent, tender lamb, goat or sucking pig.

Sepúlveda and Riaza

If you have the time, stop for some sightseeing at the historic, walled town of Cuéllar. Otherwise drive straight to Sepúlveda, which is 110km (68 miles) from Medina del Campo. Sepúlveda is a picturesque old town, perfumed with the scent of wood fires and roast meat, and it has become a popular spot for lunching at weekends. Most of its restaurants are inexpensive and unpretentious and roast very young lamb in glazed earthenware dishes.

An alternative to Sepúlveda is Riaza on the other side of the N1. Recently, wealthy Madrileños have crowded its outskirts with their weekend homes. Its centre, however, remains reasonably unspoilt, with an interesting circular plaza ringed by an arcade of quaint bars and cafés which doubles as a bullring during the town's annual fiesta. It also has some good restaurants.

Rejoining the N1 after Riaza, follow it for a short distance, and then turn west on to the N110 to Segovia. On the way, a detour to the charming old town of Pedraza de la Sierra with its old houses and cobbled streets, is an absolute must.

MEDINA DEL CAMPO
RECOMMENDED RESTAURANTS
Madrid Claudio Moyano 2. Tel: 80 01 34.
Don Pepe Claudio Moyano 1. Tel: 80 18 95.
San Roque Ctra. Madrid-Coruña Km.157. Tel: 80 06 08.

SEPULVEDA
RECOMMENDED RESTAURANTS
Figón Zute el Mayor 'Tinin' Lope Tablada 6. Tel: 54 01 65. Roast lamb. On the Plaza Mayor.
Cristobal Conde de Sepúlveda 9. Tel: 54 01 00. Ask to visit the underground wine cellar. Good views.

RIAZA
RECOMMENDED HOTEL
Casón de la Pinilla Ctra. Cerezo de Arriba. Tel: 55 72 01. Just outside the town. Very quiet and a good base for walking excursions in the area. Good restaurant.

From Valladolid or Tordesillas the route heads directly south to Madrid. There are no wine towns or wineries on this leg of the journey, but the area is renowned in Spain for its gastronomy, so a little extra driving can lead to some truly memorable meals. This is also an area of great beauty, with lovely old towns, some of which have almost been abandoned, while others seem to continue in their old ways, hardly touched by the passing centuries.

Medina del Campo

For those interested in history, it is worth making a short stop at Medina del Campo just to the south of Tordesillas. This was an important wine town in the Middle Ages, and here you can visit the castle of La Mota where the great Queen Isabella, who married Ferdinand of Aragon and thus united Spain, died in 1504.

Segovia

Segovia itself is a magnificent city, and it is worth spending some time there to visit its sights, which include one of the finest Roman aqueducts in Europe, the fascinating Alcázar and a charming Old Town or *Ciudad Vieja*.

The city is also the home of Old Castile's other great dish, roast sucking pig or *Cochinillo asado*. Again, one of the great secrets is that the animal is killed when only about three weeks old and is then roasted slowly in a large oven.

In Segovia's most famous restaurant, the Mesón de Cándido near the aqueduct, eucalyptus is burned in the roasting oven and the result is incomparable.

Further travel

From Segovia, return to the A6 *autopista*; this is a good road on which to cross the great Sierra de Guadarrama, but it should be avoided in mid-winter. Detours to the Escorial and the Valle de los Caídos, both hidden in the mountains, are highly recommended.

Riaza's main plaza, with its town hall in the centre, is the scene of an annual bullfight.

SEGOVIA

RECOMMENDED RESTAURANTS
La Cocina de Segovia
Paseo Ezequiel González 26. Tel: 43 74 62. Good wine list. Sophisticated.
Mesón de Cándido
Azoquejo 5. Tel: 42 81 03. Traditional Castilian cuisine.
Mesón Duque Cervantes 12. Tel: 43 05 37. Has been in business for over a century.

Food and Festivals of Old Castile

The Mesón La Fragua in Valladolid (see page 53 for details) is one of the best and most typical of Old Castile's restaurants. It still has its traditional large asador or roasting oven in which to prepare regional foods.

FOOD SPECIALITIES

Sopa de Ajo A garlic soup thickened with breadcrumbs, with an egg broken into the centre.

Cachelada Leónesa A hearty stew of *chorizos* and potatoes, not unlike *Patatas a la Riojana* from the Rioja. Different types of *chorizo* are used, but the most famous is from El Bierzo in the North of León.

Judías con Pie y Oreja Different types of *chorizo* and morcilla simply combined with white beans and pork (pig's foot and ear), popular around Segovia.

Huevos fritos con Morcilla de Sayago Fried eggs with black pudding, a good dish from around Zamora.

Estofado de Ternera a la Zamorana A delicious veal stew cooked with carrots, peas, onions and peppers, enriched with white wine and *aguardiente*.

Menestra a la Palentina A vegetable stew, best when the vegetables are young and tender. In the most sophisticated version of the dish, slices of chicken and bacon are added to the artichokes, courgettes, peas, potatoes and broad beans, and the stew is cooked in white wine.

Perdices a la Segoviana This is the typical way of cooking small game in the region. The partridges are baked in an earthenware dish, with vegetables.

Ropa Vieja (Old Clothes) Another characteristic stew from the kitchens of Old Castile made with cooked meat (chicken, pork, beef or a mixture of meats) with beans, chickpeas and a *sofrito* of fried onions, peppers and aubergines.

Rape Castellano Angler fish in a thick sauce made with onions, pine nuts and eggs. A more sophisticated version also has clams.

FESTIVALS

Old Castile has no great wine fiestas like those of the Rioja or Jerez, but most of the towns of the region have their annual fiesta. Bulls take pride of place here and bullfights can be colourful spectacles for those who can stomach them.

The most famous is the *Toro de la Vega* September fiesta in Tordesillas, which is said to have been started by Joanna the Mad, who watched it from Santa Clara. A bull is released in the town's central square and is then chased out on to the plain (*Vega*) where it is killed by the men of the town on horseback.

CUISINE OF OLD CASTILE

The high *meseta* (plateau) of Old Castile suffers from particularly cold winters. So it will come as no surprise that the cuisine is hearty.

Meat dishes
Meat and meat products, such as the spicy sausage *chorizo* (the best of which is said to come from León) and *morcilla* (a type of black pudding), play a central role in the region's great stews such as *Cachelada* and *Ropa Vieja* (see recommended food specialities, facing page). These may be combined both with meat and beans, and with fried eggs.

The region also produces good roasting meats – lamb, sucking pig (*Cochinillo asado*) and even kid, though this is more difficult to find.

The northern part of the region between León and Valladolid produces wonderful round loaves with golden crusts and delicious soft white insides.

The area to the north of the Duero, known as the *Tierra de Campos* ('the Land of Fields') grows excellent vegetables, the basis of the *Menestra*. Small game, particularly partridges, quail and hare, is also abundant and is usually cooked in its own juices in an earthenware dish with vegetables.

Fish dishes
As the region is far from the coast, salt water fish is rare. Occasionally salt cod is offered, usually prepared in the oven. *Bacalao a la Tranca*, which is cooked with vegetables and spices, is an interesting version. But restaurants more usually have river fish, particularly trout, which can be excellent in León and Segovia.

Castilians prepare trout in a simpler way than that of Navarra, where this is also a well-known dish – a little pork fat is used for basting, and the fish is simply grilled.

It is harder to find river crabs but well worth the search. When cooked with tomatoes and brandy they are quite delicious (*Cangrejos de Río*).

Along with roast lamb, roast sucking pig is a speciality in Old Castile. The meats are displayed here with a classic range of regional vegetables.

Galicia

Galicia is a long way from any of Spain's other leading wine regions, at least three hours hard driving from León and further from Valladolid or the Rioja. But no motoring tour of the country can be complete without a visit to Santiago de Compostela. The intention here is to guide the reader through the wine country to the south of the city and particularly the *Denominación* of Rías Baixas, which has established itself as the leading one of the province.

And Galicia is well worth a visit. It is one of the most beautiful corners of Spain, a land of sea lochs (known as *rías*), fast-running streams, winding mountainous roads and misty river valleys. Because they are made from rare grape varieties, its wines are interesting and unusual and its seafood is superb. But be prepared. Galicia's climate is milder than that of central Spain but it is also very much wetter. Try and go during the summer months – or take a raincoat.

Rías Baixas

From Santiago take either the N550 (no tolls) or the A9 (tolls) southwards until you reach the town of Caldas de Reis. The N640 and C550 then lead you to the lovely port of Cambados, around which there are several interesting bodegas.

Next day continue along the C550 along the coast until Pontevedra. The N550 and A9 will then take you further south to Tui on the Portuguese border. From Tui take the C550 (again!) westwards to visit the bodegas of the sub-zone of O Rosal. Then backtrack along the same road and drive eastwards towards Salvaterra de Miño to visit those of the Condado.

The Ribeiro

From Salvaterra you can continue along the Miño river on the PO400 to Ribadavia, the capital of the Ribeiro. Alternatively take the PO403 and join the wider N120. The same road then leads into Old Castile.

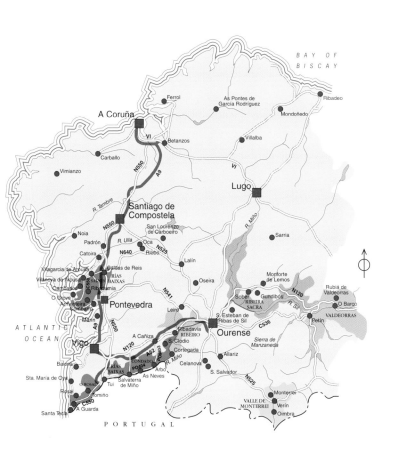

The *Ruta del Vino*

The denomination of Rías Baixas is the only one in Spain to have an organized wine route or *Ruta do Viño* as it is known in Galician. Some 40 bodegas take part in the scheme and their locality is indicated (often none too clearly) by a signpost depicting a wine glass. And these have become as much part of the landscape of the region as the famous *horreos*, the raised pagoda-like corn stores, and *cruceiros*, the crosses on the side of the road.

The Ruta bodegas are open every day except public holidays including week-ends. Some of them, but by no means all, are listed in the blue panels. Some that do not take part in the scheme but are worth visiting are also listed, although they tend to be more difficult to visit.

There is a very useful brochure (*Ruta del Vino de la D.O. Rías Baixas*) about the route, which you should be able to obtain at most bodegas. As well as providing maps giving the location of all these bodegas, the brochure is an invaluable guide to other places of interest along the route such as churches, castles and archeological sites.

SANTIAGO DE COMPOSTELA

RECOMMENDED RESTAURANTS

There are many good restaurants in this city, the most famous being:
Casa Vilas Rosalía de Castro 88. Tel: 59 10 00.
Don Gafeiros Rua Nova 23. Tel: 58 38 94.

If you want a relaxed, unpretentious atmosphere and good food at fair prices try:
O Papa Upa Clle. Raíña 18. Tel: 56 65 98.

For a drink in atmospheric surroundings try:
Cafeteria Paradiso Rua del Villar 29.

The wines of Galicia

Galicia now has five denominations of origin: Rías Baixas along the Atlantic coast; the Valle de Monterrei in the south-east along the border with Portugal; Valdeorras in the east of the province; and the Ribeiro and Ribeira Sacra in the centre.

And yet just 20 years ago very few people in other parts of Spain, let alone abroad, had even heard of these regions, let alone tasted any of their wines. The wines of Galicia were for the Galicians and a few *aficionados* that were in the know.

The Albariño grape is traditionally planted on pergolas, supported by granite posts, to get maximum exposure to the sun. This vineyard is near Salvaterra de Miño in the Condado do Tea sub-zone of Rías Baixas.

The autochthonous grape varieties

When Spain's wine revolution started to gather momentum in the 1970s and '80s, however, the Galicians soon realized that they were sitting on a treasure trove.

People in Spain and abroad were looking for young, fresh and fruity whites with character. At the time much of what Galicia produced was made from inferior grape varieties and was of poor quality. But it also produced smaller quantities of much better wine from its autochthonous or indigenous varieties, such as the Albariño, the Godello or the Treixadura, which were ideally suited to the new fashion. As they were made from different varieties, they could also stand out from the young Viuras and Parelladas being produced in ever increasing quantities in other parts of the country.

The investment boom

First, however, the region had to invest in its infrastructure to be able to produce enough autochthonous varieties to meet demand and to be able to vinify them correctly. And investment, much of it generated by the Galician business community itself, began to pour into parts of the region, particularly into the area now delimited as Rías Baixas.

New wineries with stainless steel fermentation tanks, modern crushers and new bottling lines were built while existing ones were re-equipped. The Palomino, a high-yield grape unsuited to the region but which had been widely planted in the area since the phylloxera, began to be grubbed up and replaced with autochthonous varieties. New, better sited and more efficiently laid out vineyards were planted.

By 1988 there were enough high-quality vineyards in the Rías Baixas for it to be granted D.O. status. And it soon began to outshine the province's two older denominations – the Ribeiro and Valdeorras, despite their longer history. In Spain today Rías Baixas' reputation is as high, if not higher, as that of any other white wine D.O. in the country.

Rías Baixas

The Denomination is divided into three sub-zones: the Val do Salnés around Cambados; O Rosal on the northern bank of the Miño river from the Atlantic coast to the town of Tui; and the Condado do Tea which runs eastwards from Tui along the Miño valley to Cortegada.

In Salnés, wine is made entirely from the Albariño, but other varieties are used in Rosal and the Condado, principally the Loureira in the first and the Treixadura in the second. These

and other permitted varieties such as the Caiño, however, usually make up only a small percentage of the total blend. So the quality of Rías Baixas' wines is based primarily on the character of the Albariño and on its particular development in Galicia's humid but benign climate.

The Albariño

There is a legend that the Albariño is descended from the Riesling and was first brought to this part of the Iberian peninsula by German monks on a pilgrimage to Santiago. This theory may be fanciful, but the two varieties do have some common characteristics.

The Albariño is a thin-skinned grape usually planted *en parra* or on pergolas in Galicia to give it maximum exposure to the sun. It still, however, yields wines that are comparatively light in alcohol and high in acidity.

This makes them crisp and fresh and provides balance for the high level of delicate, complex and often honeyed fruitiness that is the wine's hallmark.

Usually it is drunk when young. But more and more bodegas are now experimenting with a few months of oak ageing. This does give them an extra dimension but it spoils their raciness and masks their delicate fruitiness. The main problem is that the Albariño does tend to be light in aromas. In the southern sub-zones, therefore, the Treixadura and the Loureira are added to give the wines greater pungency.

There is another problem. The Galicians will tell you that the Albariño is the most expensive grape variety to grow in the world so its wines are by no means cheap. They are, however, undoubtedly wines of character and are well worth tasting.

Terraced cultivation in the valley of the Miño near Cortegada. Here, the river marks the boundary between the D.O.s of Rías Baixas and Ribeiro.

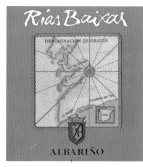

The Wine Country of Galicia

CAMBADOS

RECOMMENDED HOTEL
Parador del Albariño
Paseo de Cervantes s/n.
Tel: 54 22 50 Fax:
54 20 68.

Note that the bodegas
around this town are on
small side-roads so
directions are difficult.
Ask at each one for
directions to the next.

**Bodegas del Palacio de
Fefinañes** Praza de
Fefinañes, Cambados. Tel:
54 22 04. Fax: 54 45 12.
(Sr. Vieites). Mon-Sun
0930-1930. Housed in
17th-century palace. TP by
arrangement. WS. ☎

**Bodegas Vilariño-
Cambados** Burgáns 91,
Vilariño 36633, Cambados.
Tel: 52 44 99. Fax: 52 08 75.
(Pablo Bujan). Mon-Fri
1100-1300, 1700-1900.
E.F.TF.WS. ☎

Agro de Bazán
Tremoedo 46, Vilanova de
Arousa 36628. Tel:
55 55 62. Fax: 55 57 99.
(Cesar Silva Casal). Mon-
Sun 1100-1400, 1700-
2000. E.TF.WS. ☎

**Bodegas Castro Martín
S.L.** Clle. Puxafeita 3,
Ribadumia. Tel: 71 02 02.
Fax: 71 06 06. (Manuel
Dovalo). Mon-Fri 0900-
1300, 1500-1900.
E.TF.WS. ☎

**Bodegas Pazo de
Barrantes** Finca Pazo de
Barrantes, Ribadumia.
Tel/Fax: 71 82 11. (Adolfo
Sainz Diez). Thu-Fri 1600-
1800. No groups of more
than 10. WS. ☎

There can be few more lovely towns
from which to start a wine tour than
Cambados on Galicia's west coast.
After the touristic bustle of Santiago,
this is a quiet, charming fishing
village with a wonderful central
square, the Praza de Fefinañes, and
the ruins of the Santa Marina Dozo
monastery. The Tourist Office is just
off the main square in Rua
Novedades. Cambados also has an
excellent, centrally located Parador
and makes an ideal overnight stop.

The bodegas of the Salnés

Cambados is at the heart of the
Salnés sub-zone and a day can be
happily spent visiting its bodegas. Do
not forget that most of the region's
wineries are small and only make one
or two wines so visits will be shorter
than elsewhere.

In Cambados itself is the 17th
century Palacio de Fefinañes in the
main square which, like many
wineries of the region, produces two
types of wine, one young and the
other with a few months in barrel.

From Cambados, take the short
drive to Vilariño and the larger
Bodegas Vilariño-Cambados located
on a hill with views over the town.
Then it is again only a short drive to
Agro de Bazán, a wine estate of 11
hectares (27 acres) of vineyard near
the town of Tremoedo, with a
charismatic winery built in 1987 but
following local architectural
traditions.

For lunch either return to
Cambados or drive down to the
historic town of Vilanova de Arousa.

If you are not tired of them by
now there are two further wineries to
visit in the afternoon, both of them
near the town of Ribadumia. The first
is the small, family-owned Castro

Martín. The second is the Pazo de
Barrantes, owned by the same
proprietor as the more famous
Marqués de Murrieta in the Rioja.
The latter, however, is not on the *Ruta
do Viño* so has more difficult visiting
hours.

The alternative is to drive south
from Cambados along the C550 and
visit the magical Praia a Lanzada in
the afternoon. Along the way is the
larger, very modern but impressive
Bodegas Salnesur near the town of
Castrelo. The C550 then leads along
the coast to Pontevedra, a city that is
well worth visiting.

O Rosal

At Pontevedra get ready for a great
day out and take the N550
southwards to visit the other two sub-
zones of the region. You may want to
stop at Arcade, a port just south of
the city at the tip of the *ría* of Vigo,
famed for its oysters. Otherwise
continue down the road to the border
town of Tui (with its interesting
fortified church and a good Parador)
and turn west on the C550.

The first stop in the O Rosal sub-
zone is Adegas das Eiras which is on
the side of the road just past Tomiño.
This functional bodega is not worth
visiting but it has a roadside shop
where you can taste its wines.

From there continue to Tabagón
and then take the winding road
through pine forests to Rosal and
Fornelos to visit the Lagar de
Fornelos. Standing on the banks of a
fast-moving river, this beautiful
bodega is owned by the same
families as La Rioja Alta and
produces some of the best wines of
Galicia. You can also try its *orujo*, or
eau de vie, made in its own small
distillery.

From Fornelos visit the windmills at Folón and then have lunch in A Guarda, a town famous for its fish restaurants, and go on to the Monte Santa Tecla with its great views over the estuary of the Miño and excavations of a Celtic village.

The Condado

Two more glorious bodegas await you, this time in the sub-zone of the Condado. So drive back to Tui and then follow the PO404 past Caldelas and take the turn-off to Porto.

Overlooking its own vineyards which slope down to the river Miño, and with views out to Portugal and a medieval tower, is the 16th-century Pazo San Mauro. Ask to see the chapel, a place of pilgrimage from all over Spain, and obtain directions to the nearby Granja Fillaboa.

This equally delightful winery is approached past a medieval hump-backed bridge, stands in its own vineyards and is housed in a 19th-century stone building.

The Ribeiro and further travel

From Fillaboa, continue along the PO404 and PO400 to the historic town of As Neves and, a few miles later at Arbo, take the PO9403 to A Cañiza and then the N120 to Ribadavia.

This is the capital of the D.O. Ribeiro: it is set in lovely countryside and is an interesting town to visit. The local co-operative that dominates the denomination's production is not, however, worth visiting, so try the wines in one of the bars around the central square. Then continue along the N120 that leads back to Old Castile.

CASTRELO
Bodegas Salnesur S.A.
Clle. Bouza 1, Castrelo, 36639 Cambados. Tel: 543 535. Fax: 52 42 51. (Celestino Casal García). Mon-Fri 0900-1300, 1500-2000. E.TF.WS. ☎

PONTEVEDRA

RECOMMENDED RESTAURANT
Jaqueyvi Doña Teresa 1. Tel: 86 18 20. For tapas at dinner time.

FORNELOS
Lagar de Fornelos S.A.
Barrio de Cruces, Fornelos, 36778 El Rosal. Tel: 62 58 75. Fax: 62 50 11. (Angel Suárez Vicente). Mon-Fri 0830-1330, 1500-1800. Orujo distillery. E.TF.WS. ☎

SALVATERRA DE MINO
Pazo San Mauro S.A.
Porto, Salvaterra de Miño. Tel: 20 41 20. Fax: 20 76 08. (Domingo Villar). June-Sep 1100-1300, 1600-1900. Sep-Feb 1000-1300. 16th-century chapel and winery. E.TF.WS. ☎
Granja Fillaboa S.A.
Finca de Fillaboa, Salvaterra de Miño. (Javier Luca de Tena). By appointment only with: Finca Fillaboa S.A., Praza de Compostela, 6 ent., 36201 Vigo, (Pontevedra). Tel: 43 70 00. Fax: 43 24 64. Mon-Sat 1000-1800. Closed 1 Sep-15 Oct. Museum, chapel. E.TF.WS.

A corner of the Praza de Fefiñanes, the impressive granite-paved central square in Cambados. Among the fine buildings that surround the square is a bodega housed in the 17th-century Palacio de Fefiñanes.

New Castile

The region of Castilla La Mancha, or New Castile as it is usually known, is on the high *meseta* south of Madrid; its provinces are Toledo, Ciudad Real, Cuenca and Albacete, all of which have important wine industries.

Despite its literary connotations and the majesty of its landscape, it is a sad region, seemingly forlorn and forgotten. During the Middle Ages it was a buffer zone between the Christian North and the Moslem South. Today it plays a similar role, a no-man's-land between Madrid and Andalusia.

For the tourist interested in history or architecture, there are some splendid sites. But for the wine and food enthusiast there are fewer attractions, just the odd place of special interest hidden away in the vast, featureless plain.

This is also a difficult region to visit. Not only are the summers unbearably hot, but the distances between the leading producers are often great. Valdepeñas is compact enough, as most of its wineries are in the town, but in La Mancha, the bodegas are separated by long drives, often along appalling roads.

As it leads almost directly south, the route through New Castile is comparatively straightforward. From Madrid the busy NIV leads along a dual carriageway as far as Aranjuez, where it is worth stopping for a few hours. Then the N400 leads to the fabulous city of Toledo. The small Manchegan towns of Consuegra and Puerto Lápice are only about 70km (43 miles) further south.

From a base at Alcázar de San Juan, a day trip can be taken to the towns of Tomelloso and Villarobledo with a visit to the lakes of Ruidera on the way. From Alcázar rejoin the NIV for Manzanares, but take a detour to Arenas de San Juan and Almagro from which the C415 leads to Valdepeñas.

The flat, dusty and sparsely cultivated meseta *(high plateau) of New Castile offers awesome vistas of endless space. Most of the* meseta *is covered by the D.O. La Mancha, one of the largest delimited wine zones in the world.*

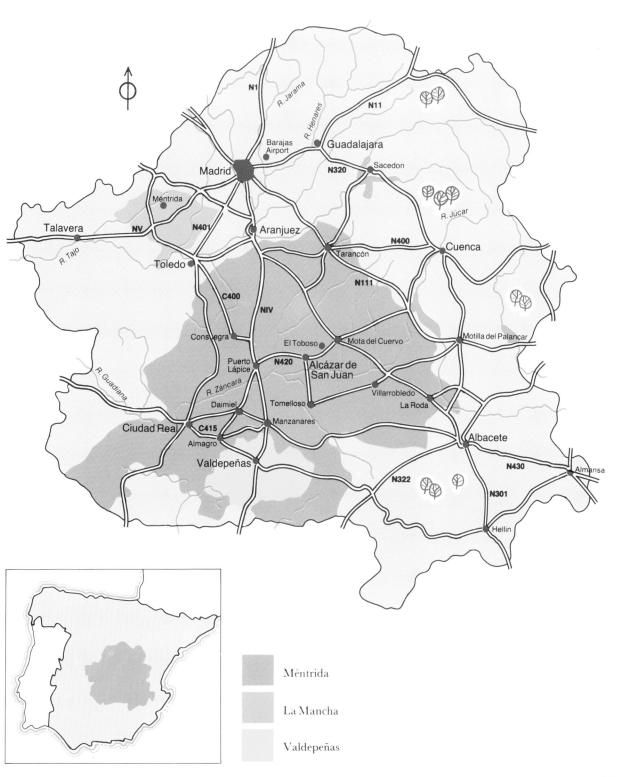

N1
R. Jarama
N11
R. Henares
Barajas
Airport
Guadalajara
Madrid
N320
Sacedon
Méntrida
R. Júcar
Talavera
NV
N401
Aranjuez
N400
Cuenca
R. Tajo
Toledo
Tarancón
C400
N111
NIV
Consuegra
El Toboso
Mota del Cuervo
Motilla del Palancar
Puerto
Lápice
N420
Alcázar de
San Juan
R. Guadiana
R. Záncara
Villarrobledo
Daimiel
Tomelloso
La Roda
Ciudad Real
C415
Manzanares
Albacete
Almagro
N430
Almansa
Valdepeñas
N322
N301
Hellin

Méntrida

La Mancha

Valdepeñas

The Wines of New Castile

La Mancha

The Denomination of Origin La Mancha covers some 176,400 hectares (436,000 acres) of vineyards at an altitude of about 650 metres (about 2000 ft) above sea level. More than half of its production, however, takes place within a 30km (20 mile) radius of Alcázar de San Juan.

The Airén covers most of the vineyard area, enough to make it one of the most widely planted grape varieties in the world. Also authorized are the white Pardilla and Macabeo and the red Cencibel, Garnacha and Moravia. Since 1996 the Cabernet Sauvignon and Merlot have also been allowed but their plantings are still small. In 1996 the production of sparkling wines, made by the *Metodo Tradicional*, the Cava method, was also authorized for the first time.

Valdepeñas

The D.O. Valdepeñas covers about 32,700 hectares (about 80,000 acres) in the southern part of the province of Ciudad Real. The Airén is also the leading variety, but the Cencibel, the only other authorized variety, is gaining ground and now covers over 5000 hectares (about 12,5000 acres).

Divided into three Denominations – Méntrida (a region in the province of Toledo, best known for its thick blending wines), Valdepeñas and La Mancha – New Castile produces an immense amount of wine. In normal years it accounts for about 40 per cent of Spain's total production, a percentage that can rise to 50 per cent when the harvests of the North are small. In area, La Mancha is the largest delimited wine region in the world, producing, in a good year, over 700,000 tons of grapes.

Spain's ugly duckling

La Mancha's wine industry is, however, very much under pressure. The acute drought of the early 1990s drastically reduced production, a tragedy for a one-crop agricultural region. And the necessity to reduce the wine glut of the European Union means that a sword of Damocles hangs over thousands of hectares of vineyards.

There is no doubt that a lot of very bad wine has come out of the region in the past simply because, up to the mid-1980s, it locked itself into a downward quality spiral. Much of its wine was sold off cheaply either in bulk to other regions or for distillation (it supplies much of the grape spirit used in the production of Brandy de Jerez, for example). This earned the region a living of sorts but it did not generate the profits needed to keep its production base up to date.

To this must be added the weakness of the Airén grape. When overpressed in the region's obsolete crushers and fermented with no regard for temperature control, this variety produced bland, lifeless wines that were, and sometimes still are,

unpleasantly sour. By the beginning of the 1980s the region had earned its reputation as the ugly duckling of the Spanish wine industry.

The advantages

La Mancha, however, does have its advantages. In good years it can produce vast quantities of wine very cheaply indeed. As there is no shortage of space, the vines are planted well apart so the yield per hectare is low (perhaps 25 to 28 hectolitres per hectare). But vine diseases are all but banished by the dryness of the climate and the extremes of temperature. It is no coincidence that, in medieval times, the region was known as the *tierra seca*, or the dry land. Viticulture is cheap and simple, enabling the farmers to keep their costs low.

A new beginning

Things began to change towards the beginning of the 1980s when a small group of enterprising bodegas began to play to the region's strengths rather than its weaknesses. In the Airén they realized that they had a base grape

that could, if well vinified, produce good everyday wines in the region at a very low cost.

Encouraged by the *Consejo Regulador*, investment began to gather momentum. New, more modern crushing equipment and stainless steel tanks for temperature-controlled fermentation were installed. And suddenly the Airén's true potential began to emerge, producing light white wines with balance, a good bouquet and a pleasant level of fruitiness. Today La Mancha's whites may not be the best in Spain but they are good value.

La Mancha's reds

Progress, albeit in very much smaller quantities, has also been made with the region's red wines. Bodegas Ayuso of Villarobledo has been specializing in red wines for many years and there was a time when it bought all the Cencibel produced in the vicinity of its bodega.

Now, however, other bodegas, such as neighbouring Torres Filoso, are also looking at reds more seriously and plantings of the Cencibel and the newly authorized Cabernet Sauvignon and Merlot are growing. This has enabled some bodegas to produce some fascinating oak-aged reds that are well worth trying. Look out for those of the bodegas mentioned and those of Vinícola de Castilla and Cueva del Granero.

Valdepeñas

Standing like a proud enclave at the southern edge of the *meseta*, Valdepeñas is a smaller region, and very different in character. It has the same climate as La Mancha, giving it the benefit of low-cost production. But it is more compact, and demand

for its wines from Madrid has been strong since the 16th century. These years of steady commerce with the capital city have enabled it to invest continuously in new technology, leaving it well ahead of its giant neighbour.

Traditionally, it has been known for its *claretes*, or light fruity and refreshing reds made from a blend of the Airén and the Cencibel (the Tempranillo), often served in jugs in the restaurants of Madrid and the South. But it also produces a small amount of white wine which, with the aid of its advanced stainless steel crushers and fermentation tanks, is of a good general standard, though not exciting.

Furthermore, as the number of oak barrels has increased so too has its production of oak-aged *crianzas* and *reservas*. Silkily smooth, with a deep colour, good fruit and subtle touches of oak, these are good enough to compete with the best in Spain. When their price is taken into consideration, they are, without doubt, some of the best buys available in the country.

The barrels below belong to Rodriguez and Berger, one of the leading wine companies of La Mancha. Unfortunately, the winery in Cinco Casas is not open to the public.

Madrid, Aranjuez, Toledo

Left: A corner of the Plaza Mayor in Madrid.
Above: The ornately pinnacled Biblioteca Nacional is one of Madrid's many historic buildings. Founded by Philip II, Madrid is sited between mountains to the north, and the plateau of New Castile to the south.

MADRID

TOP RESTAURANTS
Madrid has so many restaurants that it is difficult to make a small selection. Those below, however, are generally accepted as being the city's best. They are not cheap, but you will not be disappointed. Booking a table at all three is imperative.
Jockey Amador de los Rios 6. Tel: 319 24 35.
Zalacaín Álvarez de Baena 4. Tel: 561 48 40.
Club 31 Alcala 58. Tel: 531 00 92.

Madrid and Barcelona have always vied with one another for the distinction of being Spain's most lively, vibrant city. The big difference is that Barcelona, close to the border with France, is very cosmopolitan. Madrid, almost in the exact centre of the peninsula, has remained Spanish to its very core.

Bars and restaurants
There can be few cities in the world that rival Madrid for its sheer wealth and variety of places to eat and drink. At one end of the scale, it has some of the most sophisticated restaurants in

the world. At the other it has innumerable bars, taverns and unpretentious restaurants bursting with life at all times of the year.

During the summer try the cafés and bars in the lovely, enclosed Plaza Mayor. Then go outside and all around you will find others, some of which specialize in certain tapas such as ham or mushrooms. Alternatively try the Paseo de la Castellana with its long array of outdoor cafés. Or the area around the Plaza Santa Ana.

For those interested in history, however, the most fascinating establishments are the traditional cafés

that give a wonderful insight into the city's past. Try the Café Comercial on the Plaza de Bilbao, the León on Alcalá or the Gijón on Recoletos. The last two are conveniently close to the Prado.

Aranjuez

From Madrid the wide NIV leads south to Aranjuez, a drive of about 40km (25 miles). Aranjuez has often been described as an oasis in the great dusty and dry *meseta* of New Castile. Initially its royal palaces were built as a refuge from the searing heat of the Madrid summer. Its fabulous gardens, the inspiration of the guitarist-composer Rodrigo's *Concierto de Aranjuez*, and of the paintings of the Catalan artist Santiago Rusiñol (1861-1931), are its chief attraction. And you can have a splendid lunch at Casa Pablo, a good restaurant in the city centre.

Toledo

Just a few kilometres beyond Aranjuez the N400 branches westward to Toledo. The city lacks special gastronomic interest, although there are some reasonable bars and restaurants near the Plaza de la Magdalena. But no one should miss the opportunity to see it.

Toledo stands out like a jewel in the desolate plain. The city is famous for its superb metalwork, especially swords; it has a great artistic heritage (the painter El Greco lived here from 1577 until his death in 1604); and it has an incomparable position, with its impressive Alcazar standing on the rock, flanked on three sides by the river Tagus.

Few other cities in Spain, even in Europe, can offer so much.

MADRID (cont.)

RECOMMENDED TAVERNS
If anything, it is even more difficult to make a selection of the city's taverns. These are classics rather than fashionable ones:
Cervecería Alemana Pl. de Santa Ana 6. Said to have been a haunt of Hemingway's and in the middle of one of the city's liveliest areas. Four doors down is the **Cervecería Santa Ana** which is equally good.
El Espejo Paseo de Recoletos 31. Excellent tapas. Then cross the road to the **Pabellón del Espejo** opposite with its wonderful decor and terrace in the summer.
Taberna de Antonio Sanchez Mesón de Paredes 13. An old tavern with its original decor first opened by a bullfighter and artist.
La Bilbaína Marqués de Urquijo 27. Very old with excellent tapas.
Taberna de los Cien Vinos Nuncio 17. Big selection of wines offered by the glass.

ARANJUEZ

RECOMMENDED RESTAURANT
Casa Pablo Almibar 42. Tel: 891 14 51. Central. Good Castillian cuisine.

TOLEDO

RECOMMENDED RESTAURANT
Rincón de Eloy Juan Labrador 10. Tel: 22 93 99. Hidden away in the historic part of the city.

La Mancha

The best time of the year to visit La Mancha is during October. By then the burning heat of the summer will be beginning to die down. It is the time of the wine harvest, and the time when the *Crocus sativus* comes into bloom, covering the ochre plains to the south of Toledo with what looks like a mauve carpet.

The 'Gold of La Mancha'

Introduced to Spain by the Moors, the *Crocus sativus* yields one of the world's most expensive spices: golden saffron, the spice that makes the *paella* such a brilliant dish. It is planted in other countries of the Mediterranean, but this western part of La Mancha around the town of Consuegra is the greatest source.

Consuegra is 70km (43 miles) to the south of Toledo along the C400 and, during most of the year, it is a rather drab place. Once a year, however, on the last Sunday of October, known as the *Día de la Rosa del Azafrán* or Saffron Rose Day, it blossoms into a colourful fiesta. An elected *Dulcinea de la Mancha* presides over a joyful celebration of singing and dancing, and the local girls traditionally display the jewellery that they have bought with their earnings from the harvest work.

Into the wine country

From Consuegra it is a short hop of 20km (12 miles) to Puerto Lápice on the NIV. This is another typically small Manchegan town: it is here

The famous Jardín del Príncipe in Aranjuez (see page 71) was originally landscaped for Charles IV in the 18th century.

The phrase 'un lugar de La Mancha' *(a place in La Mancha) along with the silhouetted figures of the old Don and his horse Rosinante evoke the classic Spanish masterpiece by Cervantes,* Don Quijote. *Herencia is one of many towns associated with episodes in Don Quijote's story.*

that Don Quijote (Quixote) is supposed to have been knighted by the innkeeper.

The town does have a picturesque old inn, the Venta del Quijote, where it is worth stopping for a drink. But do not be tempted into lunch as the food is no longer what it used to be. Alcázar de San Juan is only a few kilometres away along the N420.

Alcázar and Tomelloso
Book in for two nights at a hotel in Alcázar and, the next day, take the C400 to Tomelloso. This is one of the largest centres of distillation in Spain and home of two of the most up-and-coming bodegas of the region, Vinícola de Tomelloso and Bodegas Centro Españolas. Both merit a visit, as does the Posada de los Portales, an old muleteers' inn.

Ruidera and Villarrobledo
From Tomelloso make your way via La Solana, to Ruidera to see the lakes and then, via Munera, to

Villarrobledo where you can visit the two family-owned and dynamic companies of Torres Filoso and Bodegas Ayuso. Both are among the best red wine producers of the region. Then it is back to Alcázar, a long drive via the N301 and Campo de Criptana with its famous row of windmills.

TOMELLOSO

Bodegas Centro Españolas S.A. Ctra. Alcázar Km.1, 13700 Tomelloso, (Ciudad Real). Tel: 50 56 53. Fax: 50 56 52. (Miguel Angel Valentin Diaz). Mon-Fri 0900-1300, 1600-1800. Own vineyards. E.TF.WS. ☎

Vinícola de Tomelloso S.C.L. Ctra. Toledo-Albacete Km.130, 13700 Tomelloso, (Ciudad Real). Tel: 51 30 04. Fax: 51 45 15. (Maruja Gonzalez). Mon-Fri 0900-1400, 1600-1900. E.TF.WS. ☎

VILLARROBLEDO
Bodegas Torres Filoso Ctra. de San Clemente Km.3, Villarrobledo, (Albacete). Tel: 14 44 26. Fax: 14 34 54. (José Luis Torres). Mon-Fri 1000-1300. Closed Aug and Dec. E.TF.WS. ☎

Bodegas Ayuso S.L. Miguel Caro 6, 02600 Villarrobledo, (Albacete). Tel: 14 04 58. Fax: 14 49 25. (Maria Angeles). Every day 0900-1400, 1600-1900. E.WS. ☎

ALMAGRO

RECOMMENDED HOTEL
Parador de Almagro
Ronda de San Francisco 31.
Tel: 86 01 00. Fax: 86 01 50.
Housed in a 16th-century
monastery.

RECOMMENDED RESTAURANT
El Corregidor Jerónimo
Ceballos 2. Tel: 86 06 45.
Very central, housed in an
old mansion.

MANZANARES
Vinícola de Castilla S.A.
Polígono Industrial s/n,
13200 Manzanares,
(Ciudad Real). Tel:
61 04 50. Fax: 61 04 66.
(Juan Carlos Ramirez).
Mon-Fri 0900-1330. Closed
last fortnight in July and
first week Aug. E.WS. ☎

The next day, take the road back
to Puerto Lápice and then the N420
to the small town of Arenas de San
Juan. This does involve a detour but
brings you to the fascinating Larios
Museum, a well-restored bodega and
distillery where you can see just how
they operated at the time of their
foundation in 1860. For lovers of
wildlife, Arenas is also on the
borders of the Tablas de Daimiel
nature reserve.

Almagro
If you have the time, take a further
detour to Almagro. This is not a wine
town, but its Plaza Mayor is one of
the most interesting squares in the
region, and on its south side is the
Corral de Comedias where some of
the earliest Spanish plays were
performed. It also has an excellent

*These windmills, the legendary giants of Don
Quijote's story, stand in the town of Campo de
Criptana, between Alcázar and Mota.*

Parador, the convents of San
Francisco and Asunción de
Calatrava and the lovely church
of Madre de Dios.

Manzanares
From Almagro you have to retrace
your steps to our last stop in La
Mancha, the town of Manzanares.
Stuck in an ugly industrial estate
on the edge of town is Vinícola de
Castilla, one of the leading and
most modern wine companies of the
region, a high-tech winery which
produces excellent wines.
From Manzanares the NIV leads
directly south to the small town of
Valdepeñas.

Valdepeñas

Old men pass the time of day in the peaceful central square of Almagro.

The town of Valdepeñas lies just off the NIV, 25km (16 miles) from Manzanares and 70km (44 miles) from Alcázar de San Juan. Its centre, the Plaza de España, has a nice Gothic church, a shaded arcade and some colourful houses. Apart from the bodegas and cheese firms and the usual bustle of a busy agricultural town, this is about all that it has to offer.

The wine town

Valdepeñas is, however, a real wine town. For its population of no more than 30,000 people it has some 350 wine companies; it even has an avenue dedicated to wine, the Avenida del Vino, which is lined with *tinajas*, the huge amphora-shaped jars in which the wine was traditionally fermented and stored.

The wine train

Wine-making has been the town's livelihood for several centuries. By the first half of the 17th century, it had established itself as the chief wine supplier to Madrid, a position that was consolidated first by the building of the Camino Real, the road linking Madrid and Andalusia, and then by the railway that followed the same route. Completed in 1861, the railway soon carried one wine train a day to the capital, consisting of 40 wagons, and known as the *tren del vino*.

This lucrative flow of trade laid the town's strong economic foundations and enabled it to survive two great tragic events.

VALDEPENAS
Bodegas los Llanos
Ctra. Nac. NIV Km.200, Valdepeñas, (Ciudad Real). Tel: (Madrid -91) 304 32 40. Fax: (Madrid) 304 07 13. (Alvaro Martinez, Sr. Del Fresno). Mon-Fri 0900-1400, 1600-1800. Closed Aug. E.TF.WS. ☎ Note that appointments have to be made through the company's Madrid offices.
Bodegas Felix Solís
Autovía Madrid-Andalucia Km.199, 13300 Valdepeñas, (Ciudad Real). Tel: 32 24 00. Fax: 32 24 17. (Tomás Pérez). Mon-Fri 1000-1300, 1600-1830. E.TF.WS. ☎

Continued on page 76

VALDEPENAS (cont.)

RECOMMENDED TAVERN
Mesón El Cojo Balbuena
2. In the centre of the town
with excellent tapas.

SANTA CRUZ DE MUDELA

RECOMMENDED HOTEL
Balneario Cervantes
Camino de los Molinos Km.2.
Tel/Fax: 33 13 13. Located
14 km down the NIV from
Valdepeñas, this is a tranquil
spa hotel. Good restaurant.

*A computer panel controls the flows
of wine and must in Vinícola de
Castilla, one of Spain's most
advanced wineries, and a model of
Castile's new technology.*

Disaster and progress
During the Napoleonic invasion
Valdepeñas was ransacked by the
French. Then, at the beginning of the
20th century, the region was laid to
waste by phylloxera. So much wine
was already in store, however, that
its traders managed to continue their
business while the vineyards were
replanted. Today it is still a
prosperous area. Its producers have
kept up with production technology
and the leading wineries are
amongst the most modern in Spain.

The wines
While La Mancha is on the wide
open plain, Valdepeñas is virtually
in a valley (its name is derived from

valle de piedras or valley of stones)
formed by three Sierras, the Sierras
Prieto, del Peral and del Cristo.
Rising to over 300m (1000 ft), these
protect the region from the sea's
warm breezes, and it suffers from the
same extremes of temperature as the
open *meseta*. In this climate the
Cencibel grape thrives, producing
wines with greater acidity than in the
north and, importantly, with more
colour. Even when blended with
more white than red, this colour
keeps its strength, which helps to
explain the region's great paradox.
Valdepeñas is primarily a red wine-
producing region but some 85 per
cent of its vineyard area is covered by
the popular white Airén.

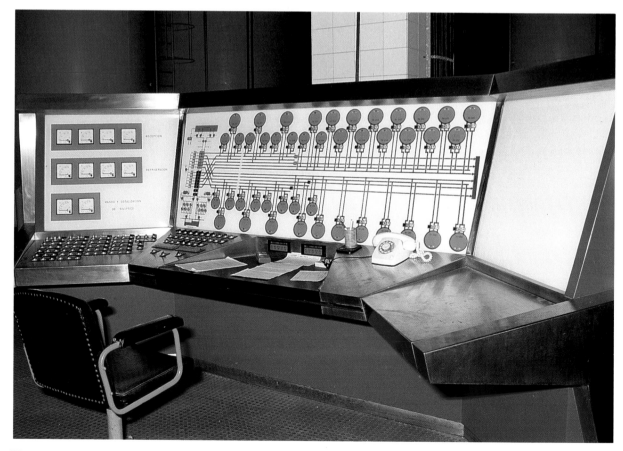

Reds and *claretes*

Traditionally, the region's famous *claretes* were made from a mixture of red and white wine. Today, however, the white must is left in contact with red grapes for colour extraction and the process produces wines that are darker than rosés, intensely fruity and refreshing enough to quench the strongest summer thirst.

In an effort to break the dominance of the Airén, the Consejo has decreed that only the Cencibel can now be planted. Production of *crianzas* and *reservas* made entirely from this grape and aged for a year or two is, therefore, on the increase, and they are wonderful value.

The town and its bodegas

In contrast to La Mancha, Valdepeñas is compact, and most of its wineries are in the town itself. There are two worth visiting. There is Bodegas los Llanos which was founded in 1875 but recently moved to modern premises on the outskirts of the town. And the larger, more picturesque Felix Solís, producer of the excellent Viña Albali aged reds, just along the road.

While in town make sure that you visit Mesón El Cojo (see panel on opposite page), an old tavern that specializes in Manchegan tapas washed down with regional wines.

Manchego cheese

Valdepeñas is also one of the largest centres of traditional Manchegan cheese-making in the country, and its production is now strictly controlled by the government. For example, it must be made from sheep's milk produced in La Mancha's four provinces, and it comes in three different styles: *fresco* (fresh), matured for the minimum of 60 days; *curado* (cured), matured for a minimum of 13 weeks; and *añeja* (aged), matured for a minimum of seven months. The result is a flavoursome, firm, round cheese of about 2.5 kilos (roughly 5.5 lbs). And it goes excellently with the local wine.

Further travel

From Valdepeñas, the wine tour heads towards the great fortified wine regions of the South. The NIV continues down through the impressive Despeñaperros gorge on the border of Andalusia to the town of Bailén with its Parador and then swings westward to Córdoba which is about 180km (112 miles) away.

Huge steel tanks store the wine at Felix Solís, one of the largest and best-known wine companies in Valdepeñas.

Food of New Castile

La Mancha's cuisine is not always the most imaginative in the country. But, in good restaurants, it can be very tasty and warming.

Dishes from Madrid

The Madrileños love wining and dining. So it is little wonder that they have developed their own special recipes, some of which have become famous throughout Spain

Perhaps the two most famous of these are the delicious *Callos a la Madrileña* which is served either as a main course or as a tapa, and consists of tripe stewed with veal, *chorizo* and *morcilla*, onions and paprika; and

Cocido Madrileño, another stew made with a mixture of meats (such as beef, chicken or veal), sausages (*chorizo* and *morcilla* again), chickpeas and vegetables such as carrots, cabbage and potatoes. Traditionally, this was served as a three-course meal of soup, vegetables and meat rather like the Catalan *Escudella i Carn d'Olla*.

Dishes from La Mancha

It is said that Philip II established Madrid as the capital of the country because it was a convenient place for his hunting parties to gather, and small game is certainly abundant on

PLAZA DE TOROS

SOMBRA

TAQUILLAS

the great *meseta* of La Mancha. Partridges are particularly popular around Toledo and form the basis of the famous *Perdices a la Toledana* where they are cooked in a pot with potatoes, garlic and wine.

Elsewhere, game is usually incorporated into the region's famous stews which were made with whatever the shepherds had to hand. The most famous of these is the very popular *Gazpacho Manchego* (see page 132), which can also be found in the Levante.

Sheep are also plentiful in La Mancha, wandering the endless plains in large flocks. Their milk is used to make the famous Manchegan cheese (see page 77), but roast lamb is also a popular dish.

Vegetable dishes
Finally, New Castile has two famous vegetable dishes, *Judías Verdes a la Española* and *Pisto Manchego*. The first is a simple dish of green beans cooked in tomato sauce with onions, garlic, spices and slivers of ham, while the second has often been compared to the French ratatouille, made with onions, courgettes, tomatoes and peppers and often including slices of ham or chicken.

*The Plaza de Toros, the bullring of the small but lively town of Alcázar de San Juan, has a grand entrance. Spectators choose between seats in the sun (*sol*) or shade (*sombra*).*

Andalusia

Jerez-Xérès-Sherry
Manzanilla-Sanlúcar de Barrameda

MONTILLA MORILES

For many people, Andalusia embodies the image that modern Spain is trying to leave behind: bullfighting, flamenco, cheap seaside resorts, Sangría and so on. But from the moment you leave the Costa del Sol there is something magical about this great, sprawling southern region. If you can avoid the tourist traps, motoring around Andalusia can be a truly memorable experience.

It can also, it must be said, be an arduous one. It is *the* region in Spain for *vinos generosos* or fortified wines, and these, together with the olive oil of the cuisine, can give head and liver a severe pounding. Furthermore, the province's three main wine regions are far apart and often linked by poor roads that make driving difficult. Finally, temperatures in the summer, particularly on the open road, can become debilitatingly high.

From Valdepeñas in New Castile, the suggested route continues south along the NIV to the small town of Bailén, and then swings westward to Córdoba. The wine country of Montilla lies to the south of Córdoba, and is reached by leaving the NIV and turning off on the N331, which leads to Montilla.

From here, the N331 continues south to Antequera and joins the N321 just to the south of the town. This excellent dual carriageway descends quickly to Málaga.

Leaving Málaga, you are faced with two alternatives. The easiest way to the 'Sherry Triangle' is along the coastal N340, which passes such famous (or notorious) towns as Torremolinos and Marbella.

For a more scenic route, the C344 branches off from the N340 just after the airport and leads to Ronda via Alhaurin el Grande and Coín and then on to Arcos de la Frontera. This is tough driving, particularly in the summer, but the beauty of these two hilltop towns makes it worthwhile. From Arcos it is a short drive along the N342 to Jerez.

Condado de Huelva

Montilla-Moriles

Jerez-Manzanilla-Sanlúcar

Málaga

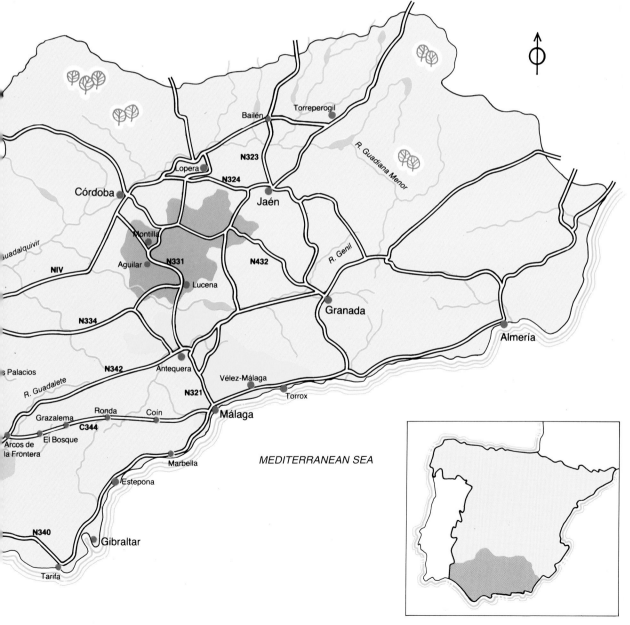

Torreperogil

Bailén

N323

Lopera

N324

Córdoba

Jaén

R. Guadiana Menor

Montilla

Aguilar

N331

Lucena

N432

R. Genil

Guadalquivir

NIV

Granada

Almería

N334

s Palacios

N342

Antequera

Vélez-Málaga

R. Guadalete

N321

Torrox

Ronda

Coín

Grazalema

C344

Málaga

El Bosque

Arcos de
la Frontera

Marbella

MEDITERRANEAN SEA

Estepona

N340

Gibraltar

Tarifa

81

Córdoba

The Denomination of Montilla-Moriles embraces some 12,900 hectares (about 32,000 acres) of vineyards. Of these, some 2900 hectares (about 7200 acres) of *albariza* or *albero* soil have been designated as a *Zona Superior*, which usually produce dry or Fino wines. The *arenas* or *ruedo* soils, composed mostly of sand with clay and limestone, usually make heavier wines or Olorosos.

Finos are normally made from the free-run must, or that of the first pressing, while the Olorosos are made from that of the second.

The Pedro Ximénez is the principal grape variety with smaller quantities of Layrén (Airén), Baladí and Torrontés.

CORDOBA

RECOMMENDED RESTAURANTS
El Caballo Rojo
Cardenal Herrero 28. Tel: 47 53 75. Very sophisticated food and surroundings.
El Churrasco Romero 16. Tel: 29 08 19. Good meat and fish in the heart of the Judería.
Círculo Taurino Manuel Maria de Arjona 1. Tel: 47 15 93. Very traditional Cordoban food at reasonable prices.

GOOD TAPAS BARS
Pepe el de la Judería Romero 1.
Casa Miguel Pl. Chirinos 7.
Casa Rubio Puerta de Almodóvar 5.

All of these are traditional Cordoban taverns.

The first stop of your Andalusian tour is the justly famous city of Córdoba. Once the centre of a powerful Moorish Caliphate and the capital of the Roman province of Baetica, it has numerous monuments belonging to its historic past: on its outskirts are the ruins of the Medina Azahara Palace built by the Moors in the 10th century; in the centre stands the Alcázar, a solid fort with splendid gardens; a sturdy Roman bridge crosses the muddy Guadalquivir; and, of course, there is the great Mezquita Mosque. With the possible exceptions of Granada and Seville, one could not hope for a better introduction to this great southern province.

The Judería of Córdoba
For the wine and food enthusiast there is an added bonus here. The old Jewish quarter or Judería is a maze of small alleys between white-washed houses. Once a year, during May, this district bursts into bloom during the *Fiesta de los Patios Córdobeses*, when the inhabitants dress their courtyards, balconies and squares in flowers.

For the rest of the year, the colour is provided by a wealth of small, hidden bars and restaurants where chilled Montilla is served with a wide variety of tapas.

An evening spent prowling these alleys from bar to bar can be a thoroughly enjoyable experience, however much one may regret it the next day. For those looking for something more sophisticated there are a number of fine restaurants listed in the panel to the left.

The sherry connection
Córdoba's great wine is Montilla, produced just to the south of the city

in the wine towns of Montilla itself, Moriles and Aguilar de la Frontera. To many it is very similar to sherry: and it is this resemblance that has been the producers' greatest headache in recent years.

Up until 1944, when the Denomination was first established,

much of the region's wine was sold to the great sherry houses of Jerez where it was, quite legally, pumped into their *solera* systems (for a fuller explanation see page 92), and eventually sold as sherry. Since then, however, this practice has been made illegal and the Montilla producers have had to stand on their own feet. Dispelling the myth that their wines are a cheap alternative to sherry has been an arduous task. But they have invested wisely, raised the quality of their wines and established a following among drinkers who prefer the lower strength of these wines.

The great Mezquita of Cordoba, the Moorish mosque dating back to the 8th century during the Moorish occupation of Spain. Along with the Medina Azahara, this is one of the greatest examples of Moorish architecture in Spain.

Montilla

Rows of earthenware tinajas *in the Alvear bodega in Montilla. The wine is transferred to these containers for the secondary fermentation, during which the* flor *develops, covering the mouths of the* tinajas.

MONTILLA STYLES

There are two basic types of Montilla, both of which are dry: the pale, light Fino, and the darker, fuller-bodied Oloroso. The addition of varying amounts of sweetening wine, however, has enabled the Montillans to produce a wider range of styles, like those of sherry (see pages 90-91):

Fino (Pale Dry) Pale in colour and dry.

Amontillado (Medium) A Fino that has been left in cask until its colour has turned to amber. Dry but fuller-bodied than a Fino.

Pale Cream A Fino that has been sweetened. Golden in colour.

Palo Cortado Between a Fino and an Oloroso. Very rare.

Oloroso Brown in colour, full-bodied, pungent, dry.

Cream An Oloroso that has been sweetened. Dark and richly sweet.

Pedro Ximénez Made from grapes that have been dried in the sun. Raisiny, almost black and extremely sweet.

Alcohol in all these styles ranges from around 14 to 22 per cent.

It must be noted that, in the U.K., the terms Fino and Amontillado are reserved for sherry only: Pale Dry and Medium are used for the same styles of Montilla.

Sherry and Montilla

There are a number of similarities between sherry and classic Montilla. Both have a basic range of styles – Fino, Amontillado, Oloroso and Cream. And, despite some subtle differences, their production process is broadly the same.

In Montilla, after the wine's first fermentation, it is transferred into *tinajas*, the earthenware containers with pointed bottoms which are stuck into the cool earth. After the second fermentation, the *flor* begins to develop, a thick layer of yeasts that covers the mouth of the *tinaja*. The *flor* enables the wine-maker to classify the wines (see also page 92). Then, after two years in butt, the wine is put through the *solera* process, a system that the Montillans claim that they invented.

The differences

Despite all of this, however, sherry and Montilla have important differences. Few people would claim that Montilla can achieve the intensity and complexity of a good sherry, but Montilla does have its advantages. It is made principally from the Pedro Ximénez grape, a variety that, in the blistering heat of the Cordoban summer, produces wines with a high alcoholic strength. Consequently, dry Montilla is never fortified and Oloroso only when it has insufficient natural strength. Montilla, therefore, is usually lighter than sherry.

In recent years some of the bodegas have also started to make lighter, fruitier wines called *jovenes afrutados* which are very pleasant and fruity when served lightly chilled.

The town of Montilla

The small town of Montilla is a mere 45km (28 miles) from Córdoba along the NIV and then the smaller N331 which winds its way through the countryside. Around the town, the vineyards can be seen planted on the famous *albariza*, a soil that has a high chalk content, is grey-white in colour with yellow streaks and produces the best wines. The town itself is typically Andalusian with the wilting heat of the sun reflected from the white walls of the houses, and colourful flower pots hung from the windows. The traveller is advised to stay in Córdoba (see page 82), but Montilla has a reasonable hotel (Hotel Castillo de Montemayor), and there is an excellent restaurant, Las Camachas, on its outskirts, shaded by big trees and built around interior courtyards with murmuring fountains. Montilla is also the home of most of the largest and most important companies of the Denomination.

The bodegas

A decade ago, there were over 20 bodegas in the Denomination. Changing habits, and particularly the trend towards drinking lighter wines, however, have taken their toll. Now there are barely a dozen left and, of these, only the venerable Alvear opens its doors to the public.

Founded in 1842, it is the largest wine company of the region. And, although its bodega in the town is only used for ageing purposes, it is set in large, well-kept gardens and, with its long dark buildings full of old barrels, it is a very beautiful winery indeed.

Montilla, therefore, is a compact, agreeable town to visit. You can drive down from Córdoba in the morning, visit the winery and have lunch. Then in the afternoon you can visit the historic mansion Casa del Inca Garcilaso with its archives and library.

MONTILLA
Alvear S.A. Clle. Maria Auxiliadora 1, 14550 Montilla. Tel: 65 01 00. Fax: 65 01 35. (Carmen de Prado). 15 May-31 Aug 0900-1330. Rest of year 0900-12.30, 1600-1700. E.F.G.I.TP.WS. ☎

RECOMMENDED RESTAURANT
Las Camachas Ctra. Córdoba-Málaga. Tel: 65 00 04.

A typical Montilla bodega, with the traditional inner courtyard, fountain and old barrels of maturing wine.

Málaga

The town of Antequera. Its castle has wonderful gardens and glorious views.

The Denomination of Málaga covers some 12,000 hectares (30,000 acres) of vineyards, although only about 1000 ha/ 2500 acres of these are used for wine grapes. In general these can be divided into two main areas: the Axarquía, near the coast around the towns of Velez Málaga and the city itself; and the higher ground of the Antequera plain. The first is planted mostly with Moscatel, the second with Pedro Ximénez.

Málaga styles

Málaga comes in several styles which vary from the dry to the intensely sweet. The level of alcohol varies too but is usually 15 to 18 per cent. The main styles are:

Seco Amber in colour, full-bodied but fermented to dryness. A comparatively new style.

Lágrima Made from the free-run juice of the grapes; dark, intense and sweet.

Pedro Ximénez Made from the grape of that name, usually darker than the Moscatel; sweet.

Moscatel Usually golden in colour. Ranging from very sweet to relatively dry.

Solera Smooth, often almost black in colour. Very intense and sweet.

From Montilla the N331 leads in a southerly direction across the very heart of Andalusia. This is a good, modern road and from it you can appreciate the full majesty of the landscape of this southern province with its pale, rolling hills criss-crossed by the precise lines of the olive groves.

Antequera, some 60km (38 miles) from Montilla, justifies a short stop. However, just before entering the town drive up the N334 to Mollina and visit Larios' winery (see page 89 for details) as it is one of the only ones still working in the region. Then return to Antequera to visit its old castle with its lovely gardens and views over the great plain of

Antequera, which lies 500m (1800 ft) above sea level, and where most of the vineyards used in the production of Málaga wine are planted. Then it is on to the N321, and a slow descent down the southern slopes of the western Sierra de Almijara to the city of Málaga.

The city of Málaga

As most tourists who land at its airport do not even bother to visit it, Málaga is still an unspoilt Spanish city of splendid gardens and tree-lined avenues overlooked by the great Alcazaba fortress. It has excellent restaurants and hotels.

Málaga is a lively, congenial place and it is best visited at Eastertime when there are magnificent religious processions and the Spanish Foreign Legion holds a parade near the port. In the eastern part of the city is the district of El Palo with an abundance of restaurants on the beach serving fish caught in the bay in the morning.

To the west is the Costa del Sol and its tourist traps but towns like Benalmadena and Torremolinos have good restaurants if you can find them.

Visit the Carihuela district of Torremolinos and do not miss the Ventorillo de la Perra in Benalmadena.

Málaga's vineyards

One of the few benefits to have come out of the phylloxera disaster is that most of the vineyards planted near the coast, which were unsuitable for grape-growing, have been abandoned.

Today, therefore, most of the grapes come from higher, cooler vineyards. Furthermore, the varieties used in wine production have been rationalized from the 30 used before phylloxera to just two: the Pedro Ximénez, planted in the higher areas, and the Moscatel planted lower down in the coastal regions east of Málaga.

The crushing and fermentation of the must is usually carried out in small, rustic wineries near the vineyards and then, by law, the wine has to be transported to the city where a more stable climate is better for ageing.

All wines must be aged for a minimum of two years in wood: some are just left in the same barrel; others, the real aristocrats, are put through the *solera* system (see page 92), which makes them smooth, more concentrated and intense.

MALAGA
López Hermanos S.A.
Canadá 10, Polígono Industrial El Viso, 29006 Málaga. Tel: 31 94 54. Fax: 35 98 19. (Trinidad Herrero, Sr. Calles). Mon-Fri 0900-1400. Closed Aug. (Groups only admitted.) TF.WS. ☎

RECOMMENDED RESTAURANTS
Café de Paris Velez-Málaga 8. Tel: 222 50 43. Elegant and sophisticated.
Casa Pedro Playa de El Palo. Tel: 229 00 13. Perhaps the best fish restaurant of the El Palo district just 5km (3 miles) from the city centre.

The rolling hills of the Andalusian interior have a strangely lunar quality. This is the homeland of the fortified wines of the South.

From Málaga to Jerez

The magnificent cliffs at Ronda hide a grisly secret – a mass execution took place here in the 1930s. Hemingway's novel For Whom the Bell Tolls *includes a description of the scene, one of many tragedies in the Spanish Civil War.*

Málaga's varieties

Málaga wine comes in several styles, from Málaga Seco, a full-bodied apéritif, to the more traditional sweet dessert wines. At their best these are unctuously smooth wines, with a raisiny aroma and flavour, and an intensity that lingers for long in the mouth.

The bodegas

When Scholtz Hermanos closed its doors for the last time recently, the Málaga wine industry lost the jewel in its crown. Now there are only two producers of any note in the region: Larios, the gin giant, and López Hermanos. Visit the former at Mollina and the latter in Málaga if you can (see page 87 for details). It is buried in an industrial estate, but it does make a comprehensive range of wines. And look out for any old bottles of Scholtz Hermanos you can find, as they are well worth tasting.

The road to Jerez

From Málaga the traveller has a choice of two routes to the 'Sherry Triangle': the first follows the coast along the N340 and N430 to a junction just before Cádiz, and then continues along the NIV; the second is a more complicated inland route.

The Costas

If beaches and resorts are what you are after, the coastal route is the obvious choice. The N340 takes you along the length of the Costa del Sol and then continues to the quieter Costa de la Luz.

The contrast between the two areas could not be greater. The Costa del Sol is Spain's premier tourist strip, an almost unbroken chain of resorts. In comparison, the Costa de la Luz is unspoilt and undiscovered. Most of its holiday-makers are Spanish, and its long, golden beaches make those of the Costa del Sol look very dull.

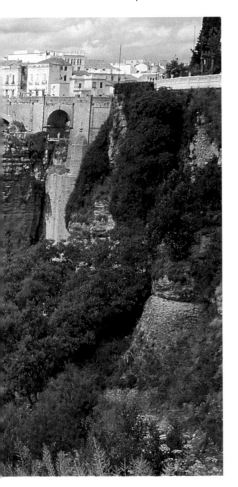

The *Pueblos Blancos*

The alternative route leads through the wild and rugged Serranía de Ronda and passes some picturesque *Pueblos Blancos*, or 'white towns', their houses with dazzling white-washed walls, their roofs a colourful jumble of sun-baked tiles.

Leave Málaga on the N340 and, just after the airport, take the winding C344 to the hilltop town of Ronda.

Ronda

Ronda is a wonderful town to visit. It is divided by a dramatic gorge bridged by the impressive Puente Nuevo; its old quarter has an interesting Collegiate church, the Palacio del Marqués de Salvatierra and the oldest bullring in Spain. And delightful gardens, set on the lip of steep cliffs, offer some breathtaking views over the countryside.

Ronda was the scene of a revengeful, hot-blooded mass execution during the Civil War. Hundreds of Nationalists were forced over the edge of the perilous gorge to their deaths, an episode which is vividly described by Hemingway in his novel *For Whom the Bell Tolls*.

Arcos de la Frontera

From Ronda the C344 continues past the pretty town of Grazalema and the National Park of El Bosque to the town of Arcos de la Frontera. Set on a high hill overlooking the Guadalete, the town has some spectacular views, while its maze of small streets and alleyways has numerous handicraft shops. With its Parador on the central square, it is an excellent place to stay the night.

From Arcos the N342 leads directly to Jerez.

MOLLINA
Larios S.A.
Appointments must be made through Málaga office: Polígono Industrial Guadalhorce, Calle César Vallejo 24, 29004 Málaga. Tel: 24 11 00. Fax: 24 03 82. (John Gallagher). E.F.

BENALMADENA

RECOMMENDED RESTAURANT
Ventorillo de la Perra
Avenida Constitución 85. Tel: 244 19 66. Housed in an old coaching house with typical Andalusian and Castilian food.

RONDA

RECOMMENDED RESTAURANTS
Pedro Romero Virgen de la Paz 18. Tel: 287 11 10. In front of the bullring.

Parador Nacional
Plaza de España s/n. Tel: 287 75 00. Housed in the Parador Nacional, this restaurant offers breathtaking views.

ARCOS DE LA FRONTERA

RECOMMENDED RESTAURANT
El Convento Marqués de Torresoto 7. Tel: 70 32 22.

RECOMMENDED HOTELS
Parador Nacional de Arcos de la Frontera
Plaza Cabildos s/n. Tel: 70 05 00.
Los Olivos del Convento Paseo Boliches 30. Tel: 70 08 11. Housed in a beautiful old Andalusian house around a central patio.

Sherry Styles

Fino

Pale and dry. The lightest and most delicate of the four styles, it varies according to where it is aged. Those from Jerez are usually heavier in body and alcohol than those from Puerto; those of Sanlúcar, nearer the coast, known as **Manzanillas**, develop a distinctive salty taste and are the driest of all. The alcohol content is 15.5 to 17 per cent.

Amontillado

Amber in colour with more body than a Fino. By nature the Amontillados are dry, but the more commercial brands are slightly sweetened.

As with the dark Olorosos, these wines gather in intensity and complexity with age, and have a distinctive nutty flavour. The alcohol content is 16 to 18 per cent.

Oloroso

Dark gold in colour, very aromatic as the name implies (*olor* means aroma, *oloroso* means pungent), full-bodied and dry. Similar in style is the much rarer **Palo Cortado**, usually described as a cross between an Oloroso and an Amontillado, full-bodied but slightly paler in colour. The alcohol content in both is 18 to 20 per cent.

Cream

This is a very British invention: an Oloroso sweetened with Pedro Ximénez wine. Dark, almost mahogany in colour, very smooth and richly sweet. A recent variation is the **Pale Cream**, which is a blend of Pedro Ximénez and Fino to produce a sweet but pale wine. The alcohol content in both is about 18 to 20 per cent.

THE D.O. JEREZ-XÉRÈS-MANZANILLA-SANLÚCAR DE BARRAMEDA

This Denomination covers some 10,150 hectares (about 25,000 acres) and embraces about 7000 individual vineyards of varying sizes. The best wines come from the parishes of Aniña, Balbaina and Los Tercios (for Finos); Macharnudo (for Amontillados); Carrascal (for Olorosos); and Miraflores and Torrebreba (for Manzanillas). The best soil is the chalky white *albariza* (see page 85). Then come the *barros* with about 30 per cent limestone and the *arenas*, sand with about 10 per cent limestone.

The Palomino grape dominates the region and covers about 95 per cent of the vineyard area. Smaller quantities of Pedro Ximénez and Moscatel are also grown. for the production of sweet wines. Their grapes are dried on *esparto* or grass mats to concentrate their sugar and produce wines that are often too sweet to drink and are used for blending in the production of various wines such as sweet Amontillados, Creams and Pale Creams.

Copitas are the slim and elegant glasses in which sherry is traditionally served in Spain. They are narrowed at the mouth to hold in the aroma.

Sherry and the Solera System

The solera *system. Butts of sherry stored in the Las Copas bodegas of González Byass in Jerez.*

The result of a happy combination of climate, soil, grape variety and the expert hand of man, sherry is Spain's only truly unique wine, produced and aged in the 'Sherry Triangle' formed by the towns of Jerez, Puerto de Santa Maria and Sanlúcar de Barrameda.

The principal grape variety

The Palomino Fino grape thrives in its warm, consistent climate, particularly on the chalky white *albariza* soil and, before fortification, it produces pleasant but not outstanding wine. It is, therefore, sherry's ageing and blending process that makes it unique.

The *flor*

After fermentation, the wine is transferred to oak butts that are loosely stoppered and never completely filled, to allow a certain amount of ventilation. Then the *flor* or flower begins to develop and grow. The *flor* is a layer of yeasts that forms on the surface of the wine and prevents oxidization by insulating it from the atmosphere. Over a period of six months it dies slowly, leaving the wine clear and ready for classification, which depends on the thickness of the *flor*.

It is another of the peculiarities of sherry that no two butts of wine develop in the same manner. The task of the master taster, or *capataz*, is to determine the style into which the wine will develop. Usually the more delicate wines with the thickest *flor* will be classified as Finos or Amontillados, while those with the thinnest will become Olorosos. Once classified, the wines are fortified and then introduced to the *solera*.

The *solera* system

The system's purpose is to produce wines of uniform quality and character. It involves several butts known as the *soleras* and *criaderas*, usually placed one on top of the other. The wine for further blending and bottling is drawn from the *solera* at ground level. Then an equal quantity of wine is brought down from the first *criadera*, and so on. Continuity in style and character is ensured by the fact that the young wine comes into contact with a far larger quantity of older wine and assumes its character.

The system has been copied all over the world, yet Spanish sherry remains unique in its subtle flavours, a great contribution to wine culture.

Jerez brandy

'The Jerezanos created art with their wine and made money with their brandy', goes a popular saying. Brandy de Jerez, whose production is controlled by a Consejo Regulador, is very different from the brandy made in other parts of the world. The producers buy their wine in other regions and often distil it on the spot before transporting it to the sherry towns for ageing and blending.

In most other regions brandy is aged by a static process, matured in a single barrel. In Jerez, however, it is put through the *solera* system in a similar way to sherry, a process known as

The bodegas of González Byass and the Collegiate Church, which dates back to the 16th and 17th centuries, are two famous landmarks in Jerez.

dynamic ageing. The transfer of brandy from butt to butt ensures that it ages faster and becomes smoother, while the addition of caramel, used in varying amounts by the different houses, gives it greater pungency, colour and depth of flavour. Most varieties also have a touch of sweetness, although some are completely dry. At the popular end of the scale the brandy can be fiery and harsh, but the premium end can offer a fascinating range that varies from the comparatively light in colour and dry to the thicker, darker and sweeter brands.

The D.O. 'Brandy de Jerez' was established in 1988. It is only the third brandy to be given this honour (the other two being Cognac and Armagnac). Strict regulations govern its ageing:
Solera Must be aged for a minimum of six months in butt.
Reserva Must be aged for a minimum of one year in butt.
Gran Reserva Must be aged for a minimum of three years in butt. In practice, however, ageing periods tend to be longer, with the *Gran Reservas* often aged for six years or more.

The Sherry Country

Continued on pages 95 and 96

JEREZ
Pedro Domecq S.A.
San Idelfonso 3, 11404 Jerez. Tel: 15 15 00. Fax: 33 86 74. *(Relaciones Publicas)*. Mon-Fri 0900-1300. E.TP.WS. ☎

González Byass
Manuel Maria González 12, CP 11403, Jerez. Tel: 34 00 00. Fax: 33 20 90. (Consuelo Garcia Tubio). Visits at 1000, 1100, 1200, 1300, 1400, 1800. E.F.G.TP.WS. ☎

John Harvey B.V.
Arcos 57, Jerez. Tel: 15 10 30. Fax: 15 10 08. *(Relaciones Publicas)*. Mon-Fri 0900-1400. E.G.TP.WS. ☎

The province of Cádiz in which the 'Sherry Triangle' lies is famous throughout Spain. For centuries it has been well known for its fighting bulls, bred on great ranches, and for its horses which are a particular passion of its people. Its fiestas, at which many of Spain's best flamenco dancers and bullfighters gather, are legendary.

Cádiz itself, set on a promontory reaching into the sea, has a splendid historic past, a fine collection of paintings by Murillo, and two cathedrals. But, on the international stage, the province is still best known for its wine. The sherry district itself, the 'Triangle', lies between three towns: Sanlúcar de Barrameda to the north, on the Guadalquivir, Jerez de la Frontera further south and east, and Puerto de Santa Maria on the coast, further south again.

Vendimiadores *picking grapes in the Albariza vineyards at harvest time in the 'Sherry Triangle'.*

Jerez de la Frontera

This is the largest of the three towns that make up the triangle. In fact it is more of a city than a town, with several good churches and other historic buildings. The 16th-century Collegiate Church (near the bodegas of González Byass and Domecq) is particularly attractive, set at the top of a wide flight of stone steps. Jerez also has a Moorish fortress, the Alcázar, dating back to the 12th century. And it is the home of the Andalusian School of Equestrian Art, which holds public displays of superb horsemanship every Thursday.

Its centre has all the hallmarks of a prosperous commercial city: office blocks, the usual mass of Spanish banks, and restaurants packed at lunchtime with smartly dressed executives. Unfortunately, it also suffers from a disease common to most Spanish cities: the encroachment of unattractive suburbs of tall apartment blocks separated by colourless, dusty streets. On the surface, therefore, Jerez is no more than a normal but busy city in southern Andalusia.

The vaults of Jerez

As usual, however, appearances are deceptive. For behind high, whitewashed walls and wrought-iron gates, there is another, almost secret world. One of long, cool bodegas with high vaulted ceilings and swept earth floors; of rows of dark oak butts with warped faces full of pungent, maturing sherry; of colourful, immaculately kept gardens shaded by tall trees; and of inner patios with tinkling fountains. It is like a hidden city, and one cannot help falling in love with it.

Historic legacies

The exact date of Jerez's foundation is unknown, but it stands in a corner of Andalusia that has benefited from a succession of foreign influences, many of which have left their mark on its towns and the character of its people. Even before the Moorish occupation in AD 711, the area had witnessed the arrival and departure of Phoenicians, Greeks, Carthaginians, Romans, Vandals and Visigoths. The Moors stayed for five and a half centuries and their influence can be clearly seen in the city's architecture. More recently, the British have established roots.

The British connection

Opinions differ, but it is thought that British merchants began to trade in

the region in the early 14th century, and the trade has been flourishing ever since.

In time, the British merchants established their own companies: Sandeman, Duff Gordon, Osborne, Williams & Humbert, Croft, John Harvey and many more, some wholly or partially British-owned. These companies adapted the product to the tastes of their clients, adding sweetening wine to make up different styles, such as Cream.

JEREZ (cont.)
Emilio Lustau S.A. Plaza del Cubo 4, 11403 Jerez. Tel: 34 15 97. Fax: 34 77 89. (Jane Ward, Maria Mercedes Orellana). Mon-Fri 1000-1400. Closed Aug. TF. Visits must be reserved in advance in writing.

A venenciador demonstrates his skills at the bodegas of Domecq in Jerez. The venencia with which he draws samples is traditionally made of whalebone and silver.

A glass-bottomed barrel (above) reveals the mystery of the flor *(see page 92). The bull (above right) is the famous symbol of Osborne S.A.*

JEREZ (cont.)
The House of Sandeman
Pizarro 10, 11402 Jerez.
Tel: 30 11 00. Fax: 30 35 34.
(Pilar Munoz Asento).
Mon-Fri 1000-1400.
Closed 27 Jul-17 Aug.
E.G.I.TP.WS. ☎
Williams & Humbert Ltd.
Nuño de Canas 1, Jerez.
Tel: 34 65 39. Fax: 32 45 97.
(Sr. Espinosa). Mon-Fri
1030-1330. Closed first three
weeks Aug. E.G.TP.WS.

RECOMMENDED RESTAURANTS
Tendido-6 Circo 10. Tel:
34 48 35.
La Mesa Redonda
Manuel de la Quintana 3.
Tel: 34 00 69.
Gaitán Gaitán 3. Tel:
34 58 59.
   All three restaurants
serve traditional food from
the region.

Great Britain became the biggest market for sherry in the world, bigger even than Spain, a position that it maintained for many years.

The British connection brought its relics of British culture too: the Polo Club of Jerez, which remains extremely popular, was founded in 1874, a mere four years after the sport was introduced to England from India (Jerez also attracted army officers who were stopping off at Gibraltar on their way to or from India); and even today it is surprising how many Jerezanos have English names.

Bodegas of Jerez
Unfortunately some of Jerez's leading companies – such as the impressive Rancho Croft on the outskirts of the town – are not open to the public. In general, however, the bodegas welcome visitors and have regular conducted tours of their premises which invariably end up with a good-humoured tasting.

The most popular of these tours are of the city's two giants, González

Byass and Pedro Domecq, two firms that personify the sherry industry. Both establishments are almost small towns in their own right, with tree-lined streets separating their numerous bodegas. In González Byass the most notable of these are the Gran Bodega Tio Pepe and the circular La Concha designed by Gustav Eiffel, the great 19th-century engineer. Domecq has the famous El Molino with a collection of ancient barrels signed by such historic figures as the Duke of Wellington, and the Mezquita, built along the lines of the famous mosque in Córdoba. Visits to

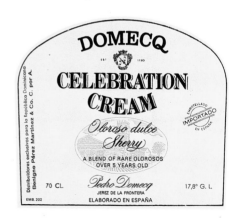

these companies are efficiently conducted but they have the disadvantage that you are often shown around in large and boisterous groups. Many travellers may prefer to visit the smaller firms.

The smaller bodegas
Try the relatively unknown but very charming and very quiet Emilio Lustau which produces a wonderful range of high quality wines; John Harvey with its gardens and small museum; or the very elegant, very English Williams & Humbert with its wine museum, founded in 1877 and probably the most charming of them all. These are just three suggestions but there are many, many more bodegas that are worth a visit.

Puerto de Santa Maria
Lying on the coast 10km (6 miles) from Jerez is Puerto de Santa Maria. In the past most sherry used to be shipped from the small docks here, but Puerto's southern neighbour, Cádiz, supplanted it in the early part of this century. From the bridge at the mouth of its river there is a fabulous view over the bay to the distant port of Cádiz.

It is much smaller than Jerez, but it is a lively little town with some first class, sophisticated restaurants, and cheaper and more modest alternatives near the railway station. An enjoyable evening can be spent just doing the rounds of its excellent *tapas* bars near the centre which buzz with life at the weekends. There are good beaches on the Atlantic, notably at Valdelagrana, and, for yachting enthusiasts, the modern Puerto Sherry marina. On its outskirts there is also the best hotel in the area (though it is comparatively expensive), the Caballo Blanco.

Puerto's bodegas
Since it is on the coast, Puerto has a different climate from that of Jerez, as it is cooled by the sea breezes and has a higher level of humidity. As a result, its dry sherries are slightly different to those reared in Jerez, lighter in alcohol and, some would say, with more finesse and a bigger *flor* aroma.

This is also a great brandy centre, the home of Osborne and Fernando A. de Terry. These are two of the leading brandy producers in Spain, the latter being as famous for its white Cartujano horses (the breed used at the famous Spanish Riding School in Vienna) as it is for its sherry and brandy. A third large concern based in the town is the family-run firm of Luis Caballero.

It is Osborne and its affiliate Duff Gordon, however, that dominate the town. El Tiro, Osborne's great brandy bodega, is on the left as you enter Puerto. In the centre of the town it has another major complex which houses its *soleras*, and is open to the public.

PUERTO DE SANTA MARIA
Duff Gordon & Co. and **Osborne S.A.** Fernán Caballero 3, 11500 Puerto de Santa Maria. Tel: 85 52 11. Fax: 85 34 02. *(Relaciones Publicas).* Mon-Fri 0930-1430. E.TP.WS. ☎
Fernando A. de Terry S.A. Santisíma Trinidad 2, 11500 Puerto de Santa Maria. Tel: 48 30 00. Fax: 85 84 74. *(Relaciones Publicas).* Mon-Fri 0900-1300. Collection of old carriages. E.TP.WS. ☎

RECOMMENDED RESTAURANTS
Los Portales Ribera del Rio 13. Tel: 54 21 16. Central.
La Goleta Babor 5. Tel: 85 42 32. In the residential part of the town.
Las Bovedas Larga 7. Tel: 54 04 40. Housed in what were the laundry rooms of a monastery.

A crested, dated barrel at Duff Gordon's San José bodega in Puerto proclaims an illustrious history in fine wines.

Three rare sherries from the family-run firm of Vinícola Hidalgo in Sanlúcar (right, from the top) a Palo Cortado, a Manzanilla and a dry Amontillado.

SANLUCAR
Antonio Barbadillo S.A.
Luis de Eguilar 11,
Sanlúcar de Barrameda.
Tel: 36 08 94. Fax:
36 51 03. (Maria Eugenia
Barbadillo). Thu 1200.
E.TF.WS. ☎ Note that this
bodega is only open to
visitors once a week.
**Vinícola Hidalgo y Cia
S.A.** Banda de la Playa 42,
11540 Sanlúcar de
Barrameda. Tel: 36 05 16.
Fax: 36 38 44. (Timothy
Holt). Mon-Fri 0900-1415.
Closed Aug. Bodega housed
in listed buildings.
E.TF.WS. ☎

RECOMMENDED HOTEL
Los Helechos Pl. de
Madre de Dios 9. Tel:
36 13 49. Fax: 36 96 50.
Housed in an old
Andalusian mansion.
Organizes expeditions to
the Coto de Donaña.

RECOMMENDED RESTAURANTS
All the restaurants on
the beach can be
recommended.
    The following are
outstanding:
Bigote Bajo de Guia s/n.
Tel: 36 32 42.
Casa Juan Bajo de Guia
s/n. Tel: 36 26 95.
The oldest of them all,
specializing in rice and
shellfish dishes.
Mirador de Doñana
Bajo de Guia s/n. Tel:
36 42 05. Splendid views of
the Coto de Donaña.

Sanlúcar de Barrameda
Sanlúcar, the third sherry town, is at
the mouth of the Guadalquivir river,
looking across at the Coto de Doñana,
one of the largest nature reserves in
Europe. It is some 20km (12 miles)
from Jerez along a small road that
leads through the heart of the region's
albariza country, and it was from this
small town that Columbus sailed on
his first great voyage of discovery, a
cause of major celebrations here in
the 500th anniversary year, in 1992.

Sanlúcar is not a beautiful town,
but it has good, modestly priced hotels
and its central square with its lively
bars is great fun. Try the Marisquería
Juan Carlos for sophistication or, for
tapas, La Gitana. Otherwise there is a
string of excellent fish restaurants
along the river with a relaxed
atmosphere. Sitting outside for a meal
of fresh, lightly fried fish with a bottle
of chilled Manzanilla is one of the
greatest pleasures of any tour of the
South. Try the *langostinos* (tiger prawns).
    Sanlúcar has other things to offer.
A visit to the Doñana park, with its
250 species of wildlife is a must, as
are visits to the palaces of the Dukes
of Medina Sidonia (one of whom led
the ill-fated 'Invincible Armada'
against England in 1588) and of the
Montpensiers, as well as to the home
of the Marqués de Casa Arizón, a
leading Indies trader.

Manzanilla
Sanlúcar's other great speciality is
Manzanilla. No one is quite sure why
this wine is so distinctive, but it is
believed that its delicious, salty tang is
the result of its ageing by the sea, a
theory supported by the fact that, if a
butt is taken back to Jerez, it slowly
takes on the character of an ordinary
Fino. Whatever the reason,
Manzanilla is the driest of all sherries,
light, delicate and with a splendid
bouquet. Also look out for the rarer
Manzanilla Pasada, a wine that has
been aged for longer, giving it greater
colour and body.

Sanlúcar's bodegas
The town itself is dominated by the
giant Antonio Barbadillo, a company
that accounts for some 70 per cent
of the world's total Manzanilla
production. Managed today by the

fifth generation of the founding family, the firm dates back to 1821. Its sprawling complex of bodegas, based around a beautiful old Andalusian mansion, occupies most of the upper part of the town.

Closer to the centre is the much smaller Vinícola Hidalgo, another family company whose charming and picturesque winery is well worth visiting.

Further travel

The 'Sherry Triangle' is where this tour through the centre of Spain ends. But if you want to continue along the wine trail, you are by no means stranded.

Anyone travelling in this region should spend a few days visiting Seville and Granada, two of the most fascinating cities in the country.

Leaving the region from Granada and heading northwards towards the Mediterranean coast, the N342 and the N340 will take you to Murcia and Alicante. The Mediterranean route described in the following two chapters can then be done south to north, reversing the directions given here.

Murcia, incidentally, is a great gastronomic centre, and the home of El Rincón de Pepe, one of the best traditional restaurants in Spain (see page 131).

The inner courtyard of Antonio Barbadillo's old Andalusian mansion lies at the centre of a complex of bodegas that dominates the upper part of Sanlúcar.

Food and Festivals of Andalusia

FOOD SPECIALITIES

Alcachofas a la Montillana Artichoke hearts served in a rich sauce of lemon and Montilla with thin strips of meat.

Estofado de Rabo de Toro Oxtail stew with carrots, peas, onions and fried potatoes.

Gazpacho Andaluz The classic version of this famous dish is also known as *Gazpacho Rojo de Sevilla*, a chilled vegetable soup with tomatoes, peppers, cucumber and garlic served with fried croutons. Two interesting alternatives are *Ajo Blanco de Málaga*, made with almonds, bread, garlic and grapes, and *Salmorejo de Córdoba*, a thicker version made with tomatoes, bread, garlic and egg yolks.

Huevos a la Flamenca Eggs baked in an earthenware dish with vegetables such as artichokes and broad beans, and *chorizo* and *jamón serrano*.

Migas Andaluzas Breadcrumbs fried in olive oil and flavoured with spices such as cumin, paprika and cloves. In the Alpujarras on the southern slopes of the Sierra Nevada, where this dish is a particular favourite, sardines and green peppers are added and it is served in a large round pan.

Olla Gitana Literally 'gipsy stew' with white beans, bread, pears and an assortment of vegetables including pumpkin and green beans.

Riñones al Jerez Kidneys with a sauce made from sherry, onions and garlic.

ANDALUSIAN FOOD

In his book *Adventures in Taste*, Don Pohren describes Andalusia as 'a gastronomic desert'. While it is true that one encounters too many restaurants where mediocre dishes are served drenched in olive oil, the food has improved greatly in recent years, making better use of excellent raw materials.

Ham, fish and vegetables

With coasts on the Mediterranean and the Atlantic, the fish – ranging from whitebait and sardines to prawns and lobster – is excellent, and can be best appreciated in the beach restaurants of Málaga and Sanlúcar. Andalusia is also the producer of the best cured ham or *jamón serrano* in Spain, coming from Jabugo, in the province of Huelva and Trevélez in the Sierra Nevada. Its top quality olive oil, almonds and sherry vinegar are already well known. Vegetables, the basis of the famous *Gazpachos*, are increasing in quality and quantity as a result of the great agricultural developments in Almería and the Guadalquivir valley, which has converted this part of Spain into the California of Europe.

Tapas

Perhaps the most charming aspect of Andalusian cuisine are the tapas, the small dishes or appetizers served with drinks, which can vary from simple plates of olives, peanuts or almonds to more elaborate offerings such as fried squid, prawns, slices of ham or Spanish omelette or *pinchitos*, cubes of spiced meat grilled on a skewer.

The perfect accompaniment to a glass of chilled Fino or dry Montilla, tapas are served in most bars of the South but are the speciality of Seville and Almería, where several of these dishes often make up a meal.

The Caballo Rojo in Córdoba's Judería is one of the city's most famous restaurants (see page 82). Its entrance is discreet and typically Andalusian, with dozens of hanging baskets of geraniums and massed potted plants decorating the whitewashed walls outside.

FESTIVALS

Andalusia is the land of fiestas *par excellence*. Córdoba has its Courtyard Fair in May (see page 82), Granada its Corpus Christi and the International Festival of Music and Dance (June and July). In Seville, the processions of Holy Week, and the *Feria de Abril*, with its frenzy of music, dancing and horse parades, are both unforgettable.

Jerez has two annual fairs that celebrate the three things that its people love best: wine, horses, and flamenco dancing and music. The first, the *Feria del Caballo*, is in May with horse racing, parades and horseback bullfighting. The second is the *Feria de la Vendimia* in September, when girls carry the first grapes to be crushed and blessed at the Collegiate Church, doves are released to the sound of ringing bells and a party of drinking and dancing begins.

Both are genuinely Spanish affairs, and are as yet untouched by commercialism.

Catalonia

PRIORAT

Situated in the north-eastern corner of Spain and looking out over the Mediterranean, Catalonia has always been Spain's most 'European' region. Its historic ties with other parts of Europe are strong, and the Catalans have tended to look more towards Europe than the rest of Spain. They have their own proud cultural heritage, their own language and a strong sense of their own national identity.

The Catalans are also good businessmen, and are said to count even while they dance. Their legendary business acumen and energy have raised their standard of living to the highest in the country and have created a strong industrial base. During the twentieth century, this development has often been at the expense of agriculture, sucking both capital and labour away from the land. But the wine industry remains important to the economy, with eight Denominations of Origin producing a wide variety of quality wines, including most of Spain's sparkling Cava wines.

As the Catalan wine regions are close to the coast, the suggested route is straightforward. From France, drive south – either jumping on and off the A7 or using the tough but more exciting *nacionales* along the coast. If you make a base on the coast you can then make one or two-day trips into the interior.

Southward from France
The A7 and the N11 cross the border at Le Perthus and lead to Figueres in the heart of the Ampurdán. For more adventurous drivers, the alternative is the winding coastal Port Bou-Roses road. From a base there it is a mere 20 to 30 minute drive to the wine country and the best of the wine towns.

To the south, the *autopista*/coast road alternative continues. From Roses the coastal road leads to El Masnou just to the south of Alella. If you take the A7 you should leave it at the Granollers exit and follow the El Masnou signs.

After Barcelona, the Penedès is about an hour's drive on the N340. A base can be made either at Vilafranca or at Sitges, a short drive away. From Vilafranca the A7 and the N11 lead directly to the city of Tarragona.

You can take a day trip to the Denomination of Costers del Segre near Lérida on the N240 to Huesca and Aragon. From there, one or two-day excursions can be made to the wine country of the interior. A pleasant alternative is to stay at either Salou or Cambrils.

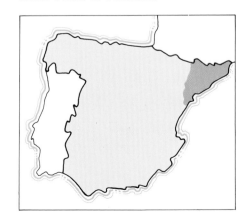

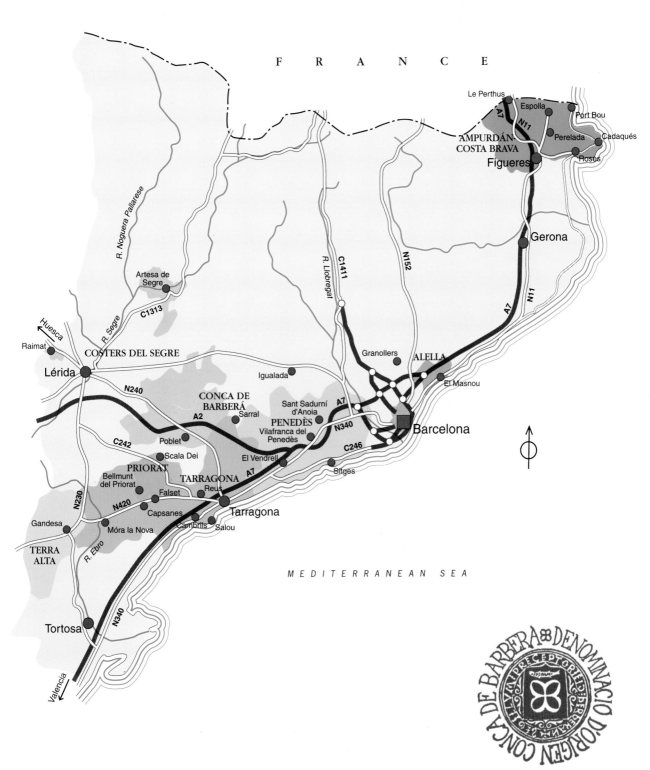

F R A N C E

Le Perthus

Espolla

Port Bou

AMPURDÁN-
COSTA BRAVA

Perelada

Cadaqués

Figueres

Roses

Gerona

Granollers

ALELLA

El Masnou

COSTERS DEL SEGRE

Artesa de
Segre

Raimat

Lérida

Igualada

Sant Sadurní
d'Anoia

CONCA DE
BARBERÁ

Sarral

PENEDÈS

Vilafranca del
Penedès

Barcelona

Poblet

Scala Dei

El Vendrell

Sitges

PRIORAT

Bellmunt
del Priorat

TARRAGONA

Reus

Falset

Tarragona

Capsanes

Cambrils

Salou

Gandesa

Móra la Nova

TERRA
ALTA

R. Ebro

MEDITERRANEAN SEA

Tortosa

N340

Valencia

Huesca

R. Noguera Pallarese

R. Segre

C1313

N240

A2

C242

N230

N420

A7

C246

N340

R. Llobregat

C1411

N152

A7

N11

A7

N11

CONCA DE BARBERA·DENOMINACIO D'ORIGEN

The Wines of Catalonia

Until recently the foreign consumer knew very little about the wines of Catalonia. Together with Rioja, Cava, the sparkling wine produced mostly in the Penedès by the *méthode champenoise*, is one of the great export successes of the Spanish wine industry. But few people outside Spain realize the quality and variety of wines produced by Catalonia's other Denominations of Origin.

An ancient history

The region's history as a wine producer is a long but chequered one dating back to Phoenician and Greek times. It was during the Roman period that the industry first began to prosper, exporting its wines with such success that further plantings of the vine were banned by Rome to protect its own grape farmers.

This strong foundation was destroyed by centuries of Visigothic and Moorish occupation, and it was not until the 11th century that a long and slow recovery began. The region was united with the rest of Spain in the course of the Middle Ages, with Aragon in 1137 and with Castile in 1497. But it has maintained a strong separatist tradition since then, an independent spirit which has left its stamp on the region's wines.

Cypresses stand guard over a small chapel and cemetery in the midst of vineyards in the Alt Penedès. This is the heartland of Catalonia's most prestigious Denomination.

Catalonia's Golden Age

By the second half of the 18th century, known as the Golden Age of Catalan viticulture, the wine industry had reached a peak of prosperity and importance. Its profits, combined with those of its satellite industries such as cork and glass manufacturing, helped to finance the growth of industry in the region. When the phylloxera destroyed the vineyards of France, the region's economy received one massive final boost that lifted exports to an all-time high and led to the planting of vineyards in virtually every adequate plot of land.

The phylloxera did not, however, stop at the Pyrenees and, by the turn of the century, it had reduced wine exports by half and left numerous grape farmers destitute. Since then, there have been periods of expansion, but, in general, the vineyard area has decreased steadily. Furthermore, in quality terms, the recovery has been uneven, with the Penedès alone being able to hoist itself to the status of one of Europe's great wine regions. This recovery has only been made possible by the success of Cava.

The Cava boom

It was in 1872 that Josep Raventós, the owner of Codorníu, opened the first bottle of Spanish Cava. The phylloxera arrived some five years later, but by then his wine had found a ready market among the prosperous Catalan middle classes. By 1877, Codorníu Cava had replaced Veuve Clicquot as the sparkling wine at royal banquets, and the industry never looked back.

Over the years this boom has generated enough profits to transform the Penedès into the most technically advanced region in Spain. And it has

MONISTROL DE NOYA 7 Febrero 1960

not been just Cava that has benefited. With its excellent production facilities and vineyards, the region also produces plenty of good 'new style', fresh and crisp whites and smaller quantities of high-quality reds.

A region of variety

Not all of Catalonia, however, has been so successful. Good wines are produced in every region, but outside the Penedès the standard is still often hampered by a lack of investment.

Nevertheless, Catalonia remains an important and varied wine-producing region: it produces Cava; it produces excellent light whites in the Penedès and Alella; lovely *rosados* in the Ampurdán; characterful reds in the Priorat; and first rate reds and whites in the Costers del Segre.

All bottles of Cava wine must have the word 'Cava' displayed prominently on their label, which may also have the words *Método Tradicionál*. The Cava cork has a distinctive four-pointed star on its base. The words *Cava Gran Reserva* on the label indicate that the wine has spent a minimum of 30 months in bottle before being disgorged.

DENOMINATIONS OF ORIGIN
There are eight Denominations of Origin in Catalonia: Ampurdán-Costa Brava and Alella in the north; the Penedès in the centre; the Costers del Segre to the west; and Conca de Barberá, Tarragona, the Priorat and Terra Alta in the south.

Together they cover over 83,500 hectares (over 200,000 acres).

By law, Cava sparkling wines can only be produced in denominated areas that include parts of the Rioja, Navarra, Aragon and Utiel-Requena. About 99% of Cava, however, is from Catalonia, with 75% of it coming from the district of Sant Sadurní d'Anoia.

The Ampurdán and Alella

RECOMMENDED WINE SHOP
Casa Ribes Pujada del
Castell 17.

RECOMMENDED DELICATESSEN
La Cuina del Gourmet
Vilatant 13. Excellent local
specialities.

RECOMMENDED RESTAURANTS
Ampurdán Ctra. Francia
s/n. Tel: 50 05 66.
Undoubtedly the best
restaurant in the Ampurdán.
Just outside the city.
Durán Lasauca 5. Tel:
50 12 50. Said to be the
oldest in the city and a
favourite of Salvador Dalí's.

CADAQUES

RECOMMENDED BARS
This once pretty and
Bohemian fishing village is
undoubtedly becoming
over-commercialized and
expensive. But two of its
bars, the **Maritím** and
Casa Anita, are worth
visiting. Both are in the
centre and the latter
displays drawings from
Dali and Picasso.

The 2977 hectares (7356 acres)
embraced by the Ampurdán-Costa
Brava Denomination are the most
northerly in Spain, and are planted
primarily with the Garnacha and the
Cariñena grapes, with smaller plots of
white Macabeo and Garnacha
Blanca. Some imported varieties
have also been planted recently but
these are still on an experimental
basis only.

Some 70 per cent of the region's
production is of *rosados*. Light in
alcohol, with a pretty pink colour,
they have plenty of fruit and should
be drunk young, as should the whites.
The region also produces some more
sophisticated oak-aged reds and some
excellent Cava.

Perhaps the most interesting wine,
however, is the fortified sweet dessert
wine, the Garnatxa d'Empordà. With
an alcoholic strength of 15 per cent,
this wine is often brown in colour, due
to its ageing in wood, and has a rich,
raisiny sweetness that is drier and less
cloying than a Moscatel, for which it
could well be mistaken.

Some firms have also recently
launched a *vi de l'any*: a wine released
in December following the harvest,
with no ageing, and in the style of
Beaujolais Nouveau.

The wines of Alella

The next Denomination down
the coast is the tiny one of Alella
covering a mere 550 hectares (1350
acres). It produces small quantities
of light reds and rosés from the
Garnacha and the Ull de Llebre (the
Tempranillo of the Rioja), but most
of its production is of white wines;
the traditional barrel-aged semi-
sweets and the 'modern', light and
young wines made principally from
the Pansa Blanca and the Xarel.lo.

In recent years the imported
Chenin Blanc and particularly the
Chardonnay have been introduced
with immense success by Parxet, one
of the two companies of the region,
and their planting has now been
permitted by the Consejo. Parxet also
produces some excellent Cava.

The Ampurdán

The Denomination of Ampurdán-
Costa Brava, which lies immediately
to the south of the French border, is
one of the oldest wine-producing
areas in the country. It is believed
that the vine was first introduced in
the 5th century B.C.; the industry
flowered during the Roman period
around the colonies of Roses and
Empúries, and later under the
ecclesiastical orders in the Middle
Ages. During the Golden Age of the
Catalan vine, it reached a peak of
prosperity when its wines were served
at the French court. Then the
phylloxera dealt it a body blow from
which it has never recovered.

Today there is still plenty of
evidence of this former glory. If you
take the steep and winding road from
Roses to Cadaqués on the Cap de
Creus promontory, you can still see
the remains of the carefully
constructed terraces on which the
vines were planted. Its vineyards
reached down to the coast and some,
so the locals will tell you, were so
inaccessible that they had to be
harvested from the sea and the
grapes transported by boat.

Today the Denomination is very
much smaller than it used to be, but
it produces good if not outstanding
wines. It is also a proud little
industry as the carefully tended
vineyards of the Alt Empordà or
High Ampurdán between the

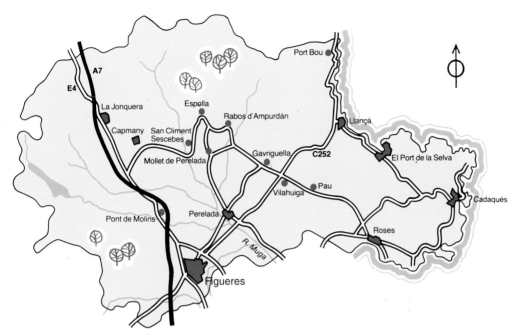

Pyrenees and the Montgris mountains suggest. Every wine town – Capmany, Mollet, Espolla, Ricardell, Pont de Molins – has a co-operative advertising the sale of wine at the bodega door. Visitors are usually welcomed.

Touring

This region is also a lovely spot for a holiday. Although on the crowded Costa Brava, it is well to the north of the mass tourist areas. With a base on the coast, several pleasant excursions can be made. Cadaqués, a small town on the coast, is well worth a visit. So too are the archeological site of Empúries and the lovely old town of Figueres. The wine country is a mere 30-minute drive from the coast and a pleasant day can be spent visiting the co-operatives and the town of Perelada, home of the leading Cavas Castillo de Perelada.

Perelada

The town of Perelada is dominated by its medieval complex which dates

back to the 14th century and consists of the Carmen de Perelada church with its charming Gothic cloister, and the Castle-Palace with its two crenellated towers. Under the church is a system of cellars where wine has been made since the church's foundation, and which now houses an interesting wine museum. The castle has a fine collection of crystal and an important library. Not to be missed.

Both the wine company and the historic buildings are owned by the same family, who have added a casino, occupying some of the halls of the old castle.

Going south

From the Ampurdán, the wine route leads south to the Denomination of Alella. As explained on page 102, you can either take the coast road or the A7, leaving it at the exit for Granollers.

Both roads should be avoided on Sunday nights, when they are busy with Barcelonans on their way home from the weekend.

PERELADA
Cavas Castillo de Perelada Pl. del Carmen 1, 17491 Perelada, (Girona). Head office (Barcelona): Tel: 223 30 22. Fax: 223 13 70. (Virginia Berjoan). Mon-Fri 0900-1300, 1500-1900. E.F.G. (all by request). WS. ☎ through Barcelona head office.

MUSEUM
Castillo-Palacio de Perelada Pl. del Carmen. The wine museum, crystal collection and library have guided tours 1100-1300, 1630-1830.

ALELLA
Parxet/Marqués de Alella Mas Parxet, 08391 Tiana, (Barcelona). Tel: 395 08 11. Fax: 395 55 00. (Xavier Cepero). Visits to be arranged in advance. E.F. ☎

RECOMMENDED RESTAURANT
El Niu Rambla Angel Guimera 16. Tel: 555 17 00.

Alella

Only a 40-minute drive from the centre of Barcelona, Alella is a Denomination that has all but vanished. It is already in the stranglehold of the city's creeping industrial estates, and its pleasant countryside has made it a prey for property developers. Today, with its 550 hectares (1350 acres) of vines, it is one of the smallest delimited wine areas in the world.

Its survival, however, now appears secure, for the grape-growers, mostly grouped into a co-operative, have stopped the granting of construction licences on delimited land, and any developments that now occur are carefully controlled.

The bodegas

A visit to the region should not take more than a day. Alella Vinícola, the region's co-operative, stands on the main road. The building's façade dates back to its foundation in 1906 but behind is a winery that belongs to the 1990s. The old oak vats and barrels have largely been ripped out and replaced with shiny stainless steel fermentation tanks, with ceramic floors and walls. It may not be as picturesque as in the past, but it is certainly efficient. And this is the only company in the region that still makes the old oak-aged wines.

Parxet, the region's other firm, has two wineries: one in Viana which produces Cava; the second in Santa María de Martorelles on the western side of the Maresme hills, which produces still wines. Of the two, the second is the more interesting, purpose-built in 1981 but attached to an old *casa de payes* or farm. This was built in the 18th century and has an original wine-making room maintained as a tiny museum.

Barcelona

Situated between the the Denominations of Alella and the Penedès, Barcelona sits squarely on the path of the north-south route. To bypass it is simple enough: it is encircled by a complete system of *autopistas*, the busiest in Spain. From the north the driver has only to follow the signs to Tarragona and Lérida (and Girona and France from the other direction) and the city can be left behind within an hour.

Since hosting the 1992 Olympics, Barcelona has come under the international spotlight and Europe has realized what the Spanish knew all along – that Barcelona is one of the continent's greatest cities. Much has been written about its cultural life. Catalonia has an artistic tradition as independent as its political one, and it has many museums, including one of Catalonian art, and much splendid architecture.

What is most striking, however, is the sheer style and vitality of Barcelona's people. This is one of Spain's most prosperous cities, and the combination of wealth and sophistication has created a vibrant gastronomic culture. In her book *The Spanish Table*, Marimar Torres estimates that the city has up to 10,000 eating establishments. Its restaurants range from the most sophisticated and expensive in the country to interesting and good value tapas bars, where you can drink and enjoy a variety of small dishes. Like all major cities, however, it has its problems. Traffic congestion is acute, particularly during the rush hour on Sunday nights, and parking is difficult. A word of warning: do not leave anything of value in your car, and carry cameras and handbags discreetly.

The Ramblas (pedestrian parade) in the centre of Barcelona tend to be packed with locals and tourists, both in daytime and at night – an evening tour of the bars here can be a memorable experience.

BARCELONA

RECOMMENDED RESTAURANTS
As with Madrid, it is difficult to single out a number of restaurants in a city with so many. The following are generally regarded as being the very best. They are not cheap and booking is advisable: **Neichel** Beltran i Rozpide 16. Tel: 203 84 08. **Vía Veneto** Ganduxer 10-12. Tel: 200 72 44. **El Raco d'en Freixa** Sant Elies 22-26. Tel: 209 75 59.

If you want a more relaxed atmosphere head towards the **Port Olimpic** district of the city near the Olympic village, where there are numerous restaurants on the waterfront.

For tapas and traditional seafood try the **La Barceloneta** district. The **Gracia** is good for bars including the **Barcelona Brewing Company** which brews its beer on the premises.

For a sophisticated, urban bar try: **El Café Academia** Carrer Llado 1.

RECOMMENDED WINE SHOP
Celler de Gelida
Vallespir 65. Extraordinary range of Spanish wines and spirits.

COVERED MARKET
For those interested in food, the Boqueria food market is one of the best in Spain, with exceptional ranges of fish, meat, vegetables, etc. Open every day except Sun. Near the Opera House and the Ramblas.

The Penedès and Cava

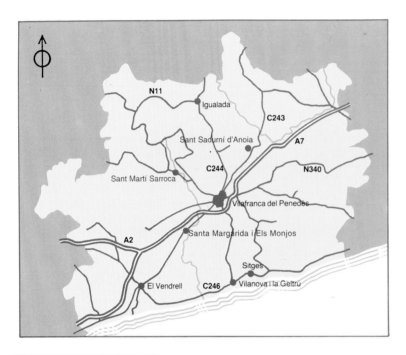

With its bursts of expansion and periods of decline, its peak of prosperity in the 19th century followed by its destruction by the phylloxera, the history of the Penedès is not unlike that of Spain's other Mediterranean wine regions. What sets it apart is its strong recovery in the 20th century. Today it is one of Spain's most prestigious white wine producers as well as being the home of Cava, one of the great success stories of the Spanish wine industry.

The success of Cava

The region has undergone great changes since the phylloxera struck. When Josep Raventós opened the first bottle of Spanish sparkling wine in 1872, red wine was still being produced here. Such was the immediate success of Cava, however, that when the vineyards were replanted, it was mostly with white

VILAFRANCA
Miguel Torres Comercio 22, 08720 Vilafranca del Penedès, (Barcelona). Tel: 817 74 87. Fax: 817 74 44. (Louise Compte Kelly). Mon-Fri 0800-1300, 1500-1700. Sat-Sun 0900-1400. E.F.G.TF.WS.

WINE MUSEUM
Pl. Jaume I. Part of a larger complex with exhibitions of art, archeology, geology etc. Housed in the Palau dels Comtes-Reis dating back to 12th-13th centuries.

RECOMMENDED WINE SHOP
El Llar del Vi i del Cava Av. Tarragona 3. Large selection of local wines. Wine tastings.

RECOMMENDED RESTAURANT
Celler del Penedès Anselmo Clave 13, Sant Miquel d'Olerdola. Tel: 890 20 01. Just outside the town on the Sitges road. Traditional local food.

One of Spain's most prestigious wine companies, Bodegas Torres in Vilafranca has preserved huge old wine presses in the bodega courtyard.

varieties. Today, red wines are produced, some of which have achieved international acclaim, but they represent less than 20 per cent of total production.

'Designer' white wines

Cava's astonishing success has had other effects on the region. Its appetite for grapes and wine is almost insatiable and many small grape-growers, wine-makers and co-operatives make a comfortable living out of supplying it. The huge profits it has generated, therefore, have percolated their way down through the entire structure and have led to enormous investment in the region's production base, which is now one of the most advanced in Spain.

The Penedès producers have other advantages. The climate is consistent, enabling them to produce wines whose quality varies little from year to year. In the Parellada, the Macabeo and the Xarel.lo, they have good native grape varieties that blend perfectly together, while the increase in plantings of imported varieties, such as the Chardonnay and the Sauvignon Blanc, help to add touches of finesse and elegance to the final wines.

The result is that the region produces white table wines that are almost tailor-made for the modern palate: pale, light in alcohol (usually 11 to 12 per cent), fruity and with a refreshing cutting edge of acidity.

Vilafranca del Penedès

While Sant Sadurní is the Cava capital of Spain, Vilafranca del Penedès, about 40km (25 miles) from central Barcelona on the Tarragona road and with an exit on the A7, is the centre of still-wine production.

The Wine Museum in the centre of Vilafranca del Penedès has the best display of wine-related artefacts in Spain. The collection includes old barrels and manual wine presses.

It is a bustling commercial town that oozes prosperity; there is a wine museum, the only reasonable hotel in the wine country (although travellers may prefer to stay at the more vibrant resort of Sitges), good wine shops and some excellent restaurants nearby. Unfortunately, it has few bodegas worth visiting.

Wine museum

The wine museum is housed in the palace of the Kings of Aragon, dating back to the 12th century. As well as having an unrivalled display of vini- and viticultural equipment, it has sections on art, archeology and ceramics, so it is well worth a browse. It also has a bar stocked with most of the wines made in the region.

SANTA MARGARIDA I ELS MONJOS

Caves Ferret Av. Catalunya 36. Santa Margarida i Els Monjos, (Barcelona). Tel: 897 91 48. Fax: 897 92 85. (José Ferret). Mon-Fri 0800-1300, 1500-1900. E.I.TF.WS.

VILOBI DEL PENEDES

Masía Vallformosa La Sala 45, 08735 Vilobí del Penedès, (Barcelona). Tel: 897 82 86. Fax: 897 83 55. (David Rovira Parker). Mon-Fri 0800-1300, 1500-1900. E.G.TF.WS. ☎

SANT MARTI SARROCA

Celler R. Balada J.A. Clave 7, 08731 Sant Martí Sarroca, (Barcelona). Tel: 899 13 56. Fax: 899 15 02. (Ramón Balada). Every day 0900-1300. Closed Aug. TF.WS. ☎
Finca Rovellats 08731 Sant Martí Sarroca, (Barcelona). Tel: 488 05 75. Fax: 488 08 19. (Sra. Cardona, Sra. Maria Luisa Esteban). Mon-Fri 1000-1300, 1600-1900. Weekend visits by appointment. Closed Aug, Dec. E.F.TF.WS. ☎

RECOMMENDED RESTAURANT
Ca l'Anna Pepet Teixidor 4. Tel: 899 14 08.

TORRELLES DE FOIX

Josep Masachs Ctra. Sant Martí Sarroca Km.7 (*desvio* Cavas Masaschs), 08739 Torrelles de Foix (Barcelona). Tel: 899 00 17. Fax: 899 15 61. (Regina Elias). Time and day of visit to be arranged in advance. Closed 15-31 Aug. Own vineyards. E.F.TF. ☎

Bodegas Torres

The leading still-wine producer of the region is the internationally famous Bodegas Torres, whose old bodega on the Calle del Comercio near the railway station can still be visited (see page 110 for details).

Under the direction of Miguel Torres, a wine-maker of worldwide renown, this firm has become one of Spain's greatest flagships, a leading exponent of the judicious use of imported grape varieties and modern production technology. A visit, therefore, is worthwhile, if only to taste the wines.

Other still-wine producers

The other noteworthy bodegas that specialize in still wines are all outside the town. The ramshackle winery of Caves Ferret, built over a honeycomb of small cellars, is on the N340 in Santa Margarida i Els Monjos and makes good young wines.

Different in style (but closed to the public) is Jean León in Torrelavid: now owned by Torres, it makes excellent Cabernets and Chardonnays in the Californian style, so look out for them, particularly now that Torres can add his special touches.

Alternatively, drive out to Vilobí and Masía Vallformosa, an attractive bodega that produces a strong range of red and white wines and Cavas from native and imported varieties.

Sant Martí Sarroca

But, for a typical Penedès winery, visit Celler R. Balada in Sant Martí Sarroca. This small but very modern bodega, all stainless steel and shiny tiles, is privately owned and makes four varietals from the traditional, native varieties and the Chardonnay.

They make for an interesting tasting and enable you to see just what each grape gives to the traditional blend.

This last visit has an added bonus. Sant Martí has a lovely Romanesque church and, from the square in front, there is an incomparable view across the rolling terrain of the Penedès, with its vineyards and wineries, to the jagged outline of Montserrat.

Into the Cava country

From Vilafranca and the still-wine producers, drive to Sant Sadurní, capital of the mighty Cava industry. The town is some 10km (8 miles) from Vilafranca along the C243 which winds its way through the vineyards.

To appreciate the size of the Cava industry, however, you should do this trip at the height of the *vendimia*. What is usually a pleasant 15-minute drive becomes an astonishing experience as you mix with the long procession of tractors hauling grapes to the crushers of the giant firms.

It then becomes easy to appreciate that Spain is one of the largest exporters of *méthode champenoise* sparkling wines in the world, with an annual production of about 37 million litres (about 8 million U.K./ 10 million U.S. gallons).

The Cava producers enjoy all the advantages of their still-wine making colleagues. They have the same consistent weather, the same advanced production base and the same native grape varieties with a sprinkling of imported ones.

This last point is particularly important to the industry, for most sparkling wine regions of the world have adopted the grapes used in Champagne. Cava's allegiance to its own varieties enables it to produce wines with a distinctive character. In general they can be described as warmer than those made in the north, earthier, with less acidity and with excellent body and flavour.

Cava

With its production regulated by a Consejo Regulador, Cava is the Denomination for Spanish sparkling wines produced by the *méthode champenoise*. The most important elements to this process are that the wines must undergo their second fermentation in the bottle in which they will be sold (as opposed to other methods, such as Granvás, where the second fermentation takes place in airtight vats), and they must be aged for a minimum of nine months before being sold.

The *removido* process

During these nine months, the bottles go through a process known as *removido* where, starting from a horizontal position, they are slowly turned until they are upside down with the sediment lying on the cork. This is done either by hand or in large racks known as *girasoles*.

STYLES OF CAVA

The amount of sugar syrup added determines the level of sweetness and the style of the wine. The very dry *Extra Brut* has less than 6 grams of sugar added per litre, and often none at all. *Brut* has 6–15 grams per litre. *Extra Seco* (extra dry) has 12–20 grams. *Seco* (dry) has 17–35 grams added. *Semi-Seco* (semi dry) has 33–50 grams per litre. The richly sweet *Dulce* (sweet), which is usually served with dessert, has over 50 grams per litre.

SANT SADURNI D'ANOIA
Codorníu Av. Codorníu s/n, 08770 Sant Sadurní d'Anoia, (Barcelona). Tel: 818 32 32. Fax: 891 08 22. (José Maria Martí). Mon-Thu 0800-1130, 1500-1700. Fri 0800-1130. Sat-Sun 1000-1330. Closed last week Sep, first three weeks Aug. E.F.G.TP. ☎

RECOMMENDED RESTAURANT
El Mirador de les Caves Ctra. Sant Sadurní-Ordal Km.4,5. Tel: 899 31 78.

In some bodegas, the removido *process is still carried out by hand with the bottles being gradually tilted until they are upside down.*

Built in the late 19th century, Codorníu's winery at Sant Sadurní d'Anoia is a superb example of Catalonian Modernist architecture, with characteristic neo-Gothic ornament.

SANT SADURNI D'ANOIA (cont.)

Freixenet Juan Sala 2, 08770 Sant Sadurní d'Anoia, (Barcelona). (Mercedes Argany). Tours Mon-Thu 0900, 1000, 1130, 1530, 1700. Fri 0900, 1000, 1130. Closed for local holidays. E.TF. ☎

Segura Viudas Ctra. Sant Pere de Riudebitlles Km.5, 08770 Sant Sadurní d'Anoia, (Barcelona). Tel: 899 72 27. Fax: 899 60 06. (Toni Miro). Mon-Thu 1000-1130, 1530-1700. Fri 1000-1130. Closed last weeks of Mar, Jun, Jul. E. ☎

SANT ESTEVE SESROVIRES

Masía Bach Ctra. Capellades Km.20.5, 08781 Sant Esteve Sesrovires, (Barcelona). Tel: 771 40 52. Fax: 771 31 77. (Santi Cardus). Mon-Thu 0800-1130, 1500-1630. Fri 0800-1230. Closed Jul. E.F.TF.WS. ☎

The bottles are then disgorged in a dramatic process called *deguelle* when they are uncorked and the sediment removed. They are then topped up with *licor de tiraje*, a mixture of still wine and sugar syrup, and recorked.

Sant Sadurní d'Anoia

Sant Sadurní d'Anoia is not the most exciting or beautiful of towns but to visit it is a must. On its outskirts is the giant winery of Codorníu, perhaps the most imposing and beautiful in Spain (see page 113 for details).

Built by José María Puig i Cadafalch at the end of the 19th century, it is a leading example of modernist industrial architecture and is now a national monument. It rises amid beautifully laid-out gardens and, beneath it, are five storeys of cellars extending for a total of 26km (16 miles) through which visitors are led on a miniature train. The winery also has an impressive wine museum.

Codorníu also owns another impressive property, Masía Bach, which produces some of the best red and white still wines of the region. Housed in an old *masía*, or country house, it is in Sant Esteve Sesrovires close to Sant Sadurní. Ask for directions at Codorníu.

Freixenet (pronounced '*Fresh-en-et*'), Codorníu's arch rival, also welcomes visitors and is located near the railway station in Sant Sadurní. It is not as imposing as Codorníu but you cannot fail to be impressed by the size of the operation which is the largest sparkling wine producer in the world.

You will need lunch after visiting these two giants and the Mirador de les Caves just outside Sant Sadurní provides the perfect location with its wonderful view over the vineyards to Montserrat.

The country bodegas

All Cava, however, is not made by companies of this size. Out in the surrounding countryside around Sant Sadurní there are plenty of smaller companies with interesting bodegas.

Visit either Rovellats in La Bleda, near Sant Martí Sarroca, with its wonderful 15th-century *masía*, or the larger but very prestigious Segura Viudas, which has an even older *masía* dating back to the 11th century.

Further travel

From the Penedès the traveller has two choices: either to follow the N340 or the A7 to Tarragona, or to take an excursion to Costers del Segre, near Lérida.

The Raimat Estate

The Denomination of Costers del Segre was only granted the status in 1988. It is a fragmented region with four sub-zones dotted around the city of Lérida and one cannot help thinking that it was granted its exalted status so as to give the Raimat estate legitimacy.

When Manuel Raventós, the owner of Codorníu, bought the Raimat estate towards the beginning of the century it was described as '3000 hectares [7500 acres] with a castle and one tree'. There was no rainfall and the land was a desert. Years of work, however, have transformed it into what has been declared by the Spanish government as 'a model agricultural estate'.

Raventós brought water to the arid land by building a canal. He flattened the nearby hills and spread their earth over his vast hectorage. And, when the soil proved to have too high a salt content, he planted fruit trees to leach it out. Today the estate has 1500 hectares (3700 acres) of land under vine and a similar area planted with fruit trees and cereals. It has its own railway station and workers' village complete with football pitch. It has an old winery dating back to 1918 and another completed in 1988 built in the shape of a pyramid with grass growing on its slopes.

Raimat produces some of the best and most interesting wines and Cavas of Catalonia. Its vineyards are planted with a wide variety of local and imported grape varieties and its winemakers have all the latest wine-making technology. A visit entails a detour. But it is still worthwhile, particularly as it can be combined with a visit to the medieval monastery of Poblet.

RAIMAT
Raimat Afueras s/n, 25111 Raimat, (Lérida). Tel: 72 40 00. Fax: 72 40 61. (Magdalena Rosell). Mon-Thu 0800-1300, 1430-1800. Fri 0800-1300. Weekend tours 1030, 1130, 1230. Closed Jul. E.F.G.I. (weekends Spanish only). TF (weekdays). WS. ☎

The vines at Raimat are trained on wires and regimented with great efficiency.

Tarragona and the Mountains of Catalonia

The Puente del Diablo, or Devil's Bridge, lies to the north of Tarragona, just off the motorway. This Roman aqueduct is one of Tarragona's great historic legacies.

TARRAGONA

RECOMMENDED RESTAURANT
El Far Muelle de Levante. Tel: 24 41 51. Good seafood and wonderful view of the harbour.

RECOMMENDED DELICATESSEN
Sumpta Av. Prat de la Riba 34. A must for wine and food lovers, with an exceptional number of wines and a wide selection of local foods. Serves breakfast and lunch.

MORA LA NOVA
Rovira, Vinícola de la Ribera Clle. Jacint Verdaguer 43, 43770 Móra La Nova, (Tarragona). Tel: 23 29 28. Fax: 24 14 18. (Jordi Vidal). Hours and days of visit to be arranged by appointment. Closed Aug. E.F.G.TF.WS. ☎

Tarragona

By comparison with Barcelona, Tarragona is a quiet provincial city with good hotels and restaurants, a fine *rambla* (parade) that leads up to a *mirador* or viewpoint over the sea and a lovely medieval quarter. If you are looking for evidence of the grandeur of Spain's Roman past, this is the place to go.

Up until recently this was also a wine city. In the 18th century, great wine trading houses established their offices near the port, as they did in Valencia, buying wine from producers and co-operatives in the interior, improving and exporting it.

Today most of these firms have either disappeared altogether or operate from their wineries in the interior. The Denomination's production is dominated by the co-operatives, which are quite happy to export in bulk while a few privately owned firms still strive to produce wines of quality. In general, however, the standard of wines in the region is very poor.

So do some sight-seeing in the city and then strike out for a day or two in the mountains.

The interior

If you are touring with a caravan, it is important to leave it on the coast. For, although the roads have been widened in recent years, the steep gradients and hairpin bends make driving very difficult. Having said that, a day or two in this remote and beautiful area is an experience that very few people will ever forget.

From Tarragona, take the N420 to the prosperous city of Reus and then continue along it in the direction of Falset. A short distance from Reus the road begins to climb, giving some spectacular views, before reaching a pass and then descending to the wine town of Falset.

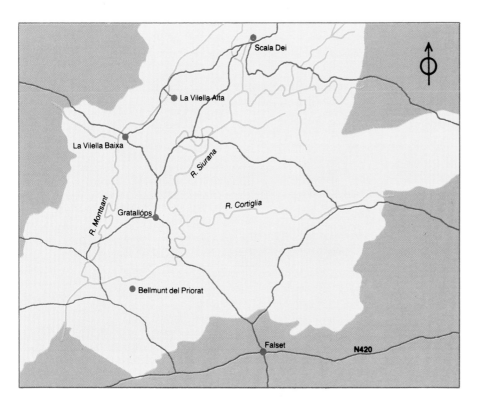

Here, we are still in the Denomination of Tarragona but the wines are very different. For, while most of Tarragona's wines are white, this pocket produces strong, full-bodied reds. And most of these are produced by the town's co-operative, which dates back to 1919 and whose winery was built in the modernist industrial style.

Rovira and Terra Alta

From Falset the N420 leads on to the town of Móra la Nova which is the home of Rovira, one of the leading wine producers in both the Tarragona and Terra Alta Denominations.

Terra Alta means 'high land' and the Denomination is on a high plateau 400m (1300 ft) above sea level. Traditionally the region was famed for its *rancio* wines, whites aged for long periods in barrel and with an alcoholic strength of over 15 per cent made from the Garnacha Blanca and the Macabeo.

Since 1992, however, new varieties, namely the Parellada and the Moscatel in whites, and the Tempranillo, Merlot and Cabernet Sauvignon in reds, have been authorized by the *Consejo* in small quantities. A new breed of wines is emerging, therefore, and one more in tune with modern tastes, lighter in alcohol and with less barrel ageing.

A visit to Rovira will enable you to appreciate both the modern and the traditional styles of the region. Then double back to Falset and spend the night, as it is one of the few towns in the area with reasonable hotels.

The Priorat

From Falset a small road leads up to Bellmunt del Priorat, and you venture into very different country. The sheer beauty of the wild, rugged terrain with

BELLMUNT DEL PRIORAT

Masía Barril Bellmunt del Priorat (Tarragona). Tel: Madrid (1) 356 2753. Fax: Madrid (1) 355 6410 (Magdalena Vicente). Visits are organized through the Madrid office. TF.WS. ☎

LA VILELLA BAIXA

RECOMMENDED RESTAURANT
Raco del Priorat Carrer Priorat 9. Tel: 83 90 65. Rustic country food in a picturesque town.

SCALA DEI
Cellers Scala Dei

Rambla de la Cartoixa s/n, 43379 Scala Dei, (Tarragona). Tel: 82 70 27. Fax: 82 70 44. (Manuel Peyra). Open all year round. F.TF.WS. ☎ Visit must be arranged in advance.

RECOMMENDED RESTAURANT
Los Troncos Rambla de la Cartoixa s/n. Tel: 82 71 58.

The ancient hamlet of Scala Dei in the heart of the Priorat (opposite) nestles at the foot of the Sierra de Montsant. The ruins of the first Carthusian monastery to be built in Spain are a short drive away and have been declared a Garden Monument by the Catalan government.

its jagged peaks and stone outcrops; the shine of its soils of decomposed slate; its decaying villages built up the mountain slopes and its abandoned lead mines that date back to Roman times make this one of the most fascinating corners of Spain.

Unfortunately, this is a region that is dying fast. Its climate and soil produce some of the best olive oil, figs and hazelnuts in Spain, and some of its most unique wines. But the low yield of its fruit trees and vines, often planted on almost inaccessible slopes and terraces, make it difficult to earn a living from the land. The young people have long since departed for the cities or the coastal resorts, leaving the region to the old, a few eccentrics and the occasional tourist.

Masía Barril

The first stop of our tour is the small, family-owned winery of Masía Barril just before Bellmunt, a bodega set high on a mountain with wonderful views over the surrounding countryside.

After the modern wineries of Northern Catalonia, Barril will come as a surprise. The owner, a lawyer from Madrid, brings the grapes from his vineyards by mule, crushes them in a tiny, antique crusher and bottles them by hand. But these are the traditional wines of the region, almost black in colour, packed with fruit, extract and tannin and with an alcoholic strength that can rise, in some years, to over 15 per cent.

There are some new wines emerging from the region, usually slightly lower in alcohol and using small quantities of wine made from foreign varieties such as the Syrah, the Merlot and the Cabernet Sauvignon. And some of these are now fetching huge prices in leading restaurants.

But Barril's wines, made mostly from the Garnacha and the Cariñena for the reds and the Macabeo and the Garnacha Blanca for the whites, are remarkable.

Scala Dei

From Bellmunt it is a 45-minute drive through spectacular scenery past El Molar and Gratallops to Scala Dei, the climax of our tour of these mountains.

Lying below the Sierra de Montsant, the hamlet served the first Carthusian monastery to be built in Spain in 1162. The small, central square is flanked by large, solid houses belonging to the four families that form the Scala Dei Association and own the town's winery, originally built by the monks. Today, however, it is well equipped with modern technology and oak barrels for ageing and produces some of the best wines of the Priorat, more accessible than the traditional ones but still very characteristic of the region.

Just up the road are the fascinating ruins of the old monastery. These were acquired in the mid-1980s by the Catalan government and there are plans to convert them into a 'garden monument'. In the meantime, with the rugged Sierra providing a suitable backdrop, they remain overgrown and mysterious.

Scala Dei also has a charming, very rustic restaurant, Los Troncos, on the road leading to the central square.

Further travel

From Scala Dei it is necessary to retrace your steps to Falset and Móra la Nova. Then join the N230 to the historic city of Tortosa (where you might want to ease yourself back into civilization with a night at the excellent Parador) and then the coastal A7 or N340 to Valencia and the Levante.

Food and Festivals of Catalonia

FOOD SPECIALITIES

Arròs Negre Literally 'black rice': one of Catalonia's answers to paella. Rice cooked in a large, two-handled frying pan with shellfish, particularly squid, which gives the dish its colour.

Escudella i Carn d'Olla A very traditional, rustic Catalan dish which is a favourite at Christmas. A veal or beef stew with vegetables, *butifarra* sausage served whole and a *pilota*, a long roll of minced beef and pork flavoured with garlic, cinnamon and pine nuts. The broth is made into a pasta soup and served as an entree.

Faves a la Catalana Broad beans stewed in white wine with black *butifarra*, and thick slices of bacon and onions.

Parrillada Fish, shellfish or meat simply grilled over an open fire and served with a variety of different sauces.

Anec amb Figues A very typical dish of the Ampurdán, duck roasted in a little brandy or sherry with figs, dried or fresh.

Sarsuela One of the classic dishes of Catalonia, a fish casserole which can be extremely elaborate. Some chefs use only shellfish such as clams, mussels, prawns and lobster. Others mix in chunks of fish such as hake.

Other stews to look out for are the *Suquet* or *Romesco de Peix*.

CATALONIAN CUISINE

Catalonia is generally considered to have the most varied and sophisticated cuisine in Spain. As is the case in most of the country's northerly regions, its chefs have a wide variety of excellent local ingredients at their disposal, but what sets them apart is the flair and imagination of combinations such as duck with figs or pears, quail or chicken with raisins and pine nuts, pork with prunes and beef with dried fruits such as apricots and figs.

Fresh ingredients

The coast, of course, produces good fish which is either served in a stew such as the *Sarsuela*, or grilled with sauces in the excellent *Parrilladas*. In addition the fertile Ebro valley to the south of Tarragona is the source of wonderful rice (combined with squid in *Arròs Negre*), fruit and vegetables. Further inland the more wooded areas yield an abundance of small game, herbs, mushrooms, particularly the unique *rovellons*, and the very popular pine nuts. Veal, chicken, goose and pork are all used, the last being the basis of the typical *botifarra* sausages, with pine nuts, cinnamon, almonds and cumin.

Catalan sauces

It is sauces, however, that are the great Catalan speciality. There is the famous *allioli*, made with garlic and olive oil; the *romesco* of Tarragona, which can be very hot, made with garlic, small peppers, tomatoes, bread and roasted almonds; *sanfaina*, with sautéed onions, aubergines, courgettes and tomatoes; and *picada*, with saffron, garlic, hazelnuts, almonds, parsley and cinnamon. These sauces are served either to accompany grilled shellfish, fish or meat, or form the basis of a Catalan stew such as the famous *Romesco de Peix*.

FESTIVALS

Vilafranca del Penedès celebrates its wine festival every odd-numbered year (1999, 2001 etc) in April or May, when wine stands are set up in the town's central square.

Otherwise, most of the region's wine festivals are in early September: the *Feria del Vino* in Figueres, which takes place in the first week of September; or the *Fiesta de la Varema* when the harvest's first must is blessed in the central square of Alella. Perhaps the most original,

from a gastronomic point of view, is San Majín in Tarragona in August which includes a *romesco* sauce competition in the Serallo district.

The most famous fiesta sight of the region are Tarragona's *Castellers* or *Xiquets de Valls*, pyramids formed by young men dressed in local costumes at the big fiestas of Reus, Valls, El Vendrell and Tarragona, and the *Fiesta Mayor* of Vilafranca at the end of August. In general, however, the region has nothing as spectacular as San Fermín, the Fallas or the *Feria de Abril* in Seville.

Participants in the festival at Vilafranca form Castellers *or human castles. These acrobatic displays originated in Tarragona, but they are now traditional in most fiestas of southern Catalonia.*

The Levante and the Islands

Embracing five Denominations of Origin – Alicante, Jumilla, Yecla, Utiel-Requena and Valencia – the Levante has vineyards in the provinces of Castellón, Valencia, Alicante and Murcia. A sixth Denomination, Almansa, which is more Levantine than Manchegan in character, is included in this chapter, although it is sometimes grouped with the neighbouring Denominations of Castilla-La Mancha.

The Levante can be divided into two parts: the interior, with the Denominations of Utiel-Requena, Almansa, Yecla and Jumilla; and the coastal stretch which includes the Denominations of Valencia and Alicante. The contrast between the two, the one with its small towns, arid mountains and gorges; and the other with its fertile plains covered with orange groves, paddy fields and vineyards, its two great cities and its coastal resorts, could not be greater and adds excitement to a wine tour of the region.

Combined with the excellent climate, the wonderful food and the great variety of wines, the contrasting scenery makes travelling in this part of the country especially delightful.

The wine regions of the Levante can be visited following one of two routes. You can base yourself in Valencia and Alicante, and then make one- or two-day excursions into the interior (from Valencia into the Denominations of Valencia and Utiel-Requena; from Alicante into Alicante, Jumilla, Yecla and Almansa). Or, and this is the suggested route, start in Valencia and then make a circular sweep through the wine regions, ending up in Alicante.

The advantages of the second route are that you avoid the crowded coast (which has some of the most commercialized and degraded seaside resorts in Spain), and that you travel through some spectacular countryside, particularly between Requena and Almansa.

Valencia is about 190km (120 miles) from Tortosa (where the tour of Catalonia ended), along the A7 or the N332, both of which follow the coast.

After spending a few days in Valencia, you can take the N111 in the direction of Madrid to Chiva and then up to the edges of the great plateau of La Mancha and the towns of Utiel and Requena.

The Sierras and Southwards

From Requena the difficult N330 leads through some fascinating mountainous terrain and then descends to the wine town of Almansa in the province of Albacete. From here you can either travel to Villena, one of the main wine towns of the Denomination of Alicante, or cross the border into Murcia along the small C3223 to Yecla and then the C3314 to Jumilla. The city of Murcia is then only 120km (75 miles) away, a worthwhile detour.

Otherwise, continue to the C3213 to Monóvar, the other important centre in the D.O. Alicante, before joining the N330 to Alicante itself.

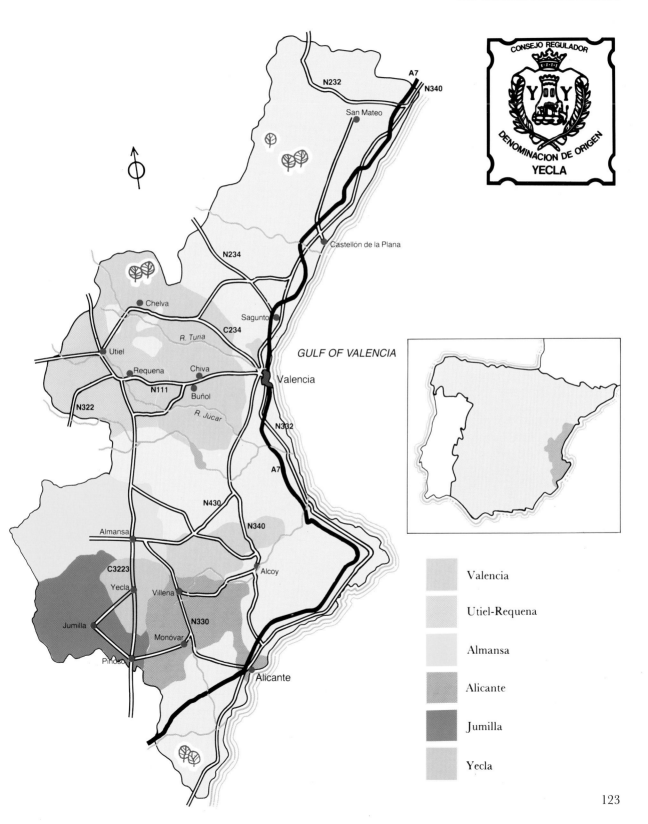

CONSEJO REGULADOR

Y Y

DENOMINACION DE ORIGEN

YECLA

N232

A7

N340

San Mateo

N234

Castellón de la Plana

Chelva

Sagunto

C234

R. Turia

Utiel

Requena

Chiva

Valencia

N111

Buñol

N322

R. Júcar

GULF OF VALENCIA

N332

A7

N430

N340

Almansa

Alcoy

C3223

Yecla

Villena

N330

Jumilla

Monóvar

Pinoso

Alicante

Valencia

Utiel-Requena

Almansa

Alicante

Jumilla

Yecla

123

The Wines of the Levante

Grape varieties

The six Denominations of the Levante cover some 164,000 hectares (about 400,000 acres) of vineyards and produce about 3,850,000 hectolitres (roughly 100 million gallons) of wine a year.

The principal grape varieties are the white Merseguera and the red Monastrell. Also authorized and planted in smaller quantities are the red Bobal (the predominant variety of Utiel-Requena), the Garnacha Tintorera and the Cencibel (the Tempranillo), and the white Macabeo and Planta Nova which is indigenous to the region. There are also some small plantings of imported varieties but these are still on an experimental basis.

The wine industry of the Levante first flourished when the Romans established themselves around the city of Sagunto at the end of the second Punic War. Periods of expansion and retraction, particularly during the Moorish occupation, have followed. But, in general, the wine industry has thrived since the Christian Reconquest.

By the 18th century wine merchants from Bordeaux were strengthening their wine with the stronger, deeper-coloured wines from Valencia, a trade that reached its climax when France was struck by the phylloxera. This boom, however, was short-lived. The French industry recovered, protected by high duties on

The vast VINIVAL winery in El Grao has been dubbed 'the cathedral', and is one of the city's best-known landmarks. It is also one of the largest wineries in Spain, with its own rail sidings.

imported wine, and the phylloxera reached the Levante in 1900.

Although the disease did not affect the region as badly as other parts of the country (Jumilla, for example, was phylloxera-free until very recently) it led to a great geographical restructuring: when the vineyards on the littoral plains were destroyed, their rich alluvial soil was replanted with citrus fruit, almonds and garden vegetables. The vines were forced inland to the arid mountains where the soil was too poor to sustain other crops. Coincidentally, they thrived in the cooler climate.

The export tradition

The phylloxera, however, did not affect the region's strong exporting tradition. For, although Jumilla and Yecla have created a strong market in the southern part of the country, the

other regions have traditionally looked abroad for their sales, a practice that dates back to Roman times when the wines of the Levante were exported all over the Empire.

This situation is beginning to change, and the region's wines are now more common on the shelves of supermarkets in Spain. But four out of every five litres of wine leaving Valencia (usually under the Denominations of Valencia or Utiel-Requena) are still destined for foreign climes. In good years some 44 million litres (roughly 10 million gallons) of D.O. Valencia wine alone are shipped abroad.

Bulk shipments

This is an impressive achievement but it disguises an important weakness. A large percentage of these exports are in bulk, destined to be blended with the wines of other countries or to be bottled under the brand of a supermarket or retail chain. Profit margins are slim, and although the producers are able to put bottles on foreign shelves at an attractive price, this generates little capital for investment. For a long time, while other regions such as the Penedès and the Rioja raced ahead, updating their wineries and improving their vineyards, the Levante stood still. It is only recently that the region has begun to invest and to modernize, and it is still some way behind the times.

Variety and quantity

This is still an immensely important wine region, however. It produces more wine than any other part of Spain except La Mancha, and its wines are varied. Recent improvements in production facilities have enabled the big Valencian firms to make a new

generation of good-value wines for everyday drinking.

The great red wine areas – Alicante, Jumilla, Yecla and Almansa – continue to produce their traditional red wines, big in body, strong in alcohol and deep in colour. These may not be to everybody's taste, but they could never be described as lacking in character. Utiel-Requena, with its cooler climate, produces some excellent young whites and rosés; while all over the region some fascinating fortified wines are made, culminating in the glorious, copper-coloured, oak-aged Fondillón of Alicante.

Valencia's great cathedral, which stands on the site of an ancient mosque in the centre of the city, has an octagonal Gothic tower called the Miguelete (literally 'Little Michael').

Valencia

Lace and mantillas are part of traditional Levantine costumery. This parade is part of the Fallas *festival of Valencia.*

VALENCIA

RECOMMENDED RESTAURANTS
Chamberlan Chile 4.
Tel: 393 37 74. *Haute cuisine* and expensive.
Marisquería Civera
Lérida 11. Tel: 347 59 17.
Specializes in shellfish.
Taberna Alkazar Mosén
Femades 11. Tel: 351 55 51.
Good tapas in the front bar
and more sophisticated
dining rooms behind.

Otherwise try some of
the restaurants on the beach
of **El Soler** or the bars in
the **Barrio del Carmen.**

After Madrid and Barcelona, Valencia is Spain's third city. The nearby port of El Grao is the largest in the country, shipping a wide range of Spanish goods abroad: clothes, computers, cars, fruit and vegetables, and, of course, vast quantities of wine. Until quite recently, the city and the port were separate, two cities in their own right. Today, urban sprawl has linked them together.

Valencia does not have the archeological interest of Tarragona, the unique architecture of the great southern cities, or the culture and vitality of Barcelona or Madrid. But it has a wonderfully relaxed atmosphere, a constant ebb and flow of sun-tanned people walking the tree-lined avenues in the evening or sitting in the outdoor restaurants and bars. The inhabitants enjoy their sunny climate and also bask in the wealth of this industrial and fertile area. Once a year, the natural exuberance of the people finds expression in the colourful festival of *Fallas* (see also page 133).

The city's wine trade

Despite its long history of wine trading, Valencia is not really a 'wine city'. In its bustling bars and restaurants the favourite drinks are beer and even cocktails. If wine is ordered, it is far more likely to be a Rioja or a Penedès than one from the region. This is the price that the city has had to pay for its export tradition and its producers have only recently begun to put it right.

The trade is dominated by four huge companies, two of them Swiss. And, although three of them own some vineyards, they are brokers rather than producers by tradition, buying wine mostly from the co-operatives and filtering and blending it to their customers' specifications.

Levantine investments

These companies represent the dynamic, progressive sector of the Levante's wine industry. They are well aware that there is a great international demand for light, well-made table wine, and in recent years they have invested heavily in their wineries, with new stainless steel storage and fermentation tanks, better filtering and laboratory equipment, and new, super-efficient bottling lines. They can now produce far cleaner, fresher and fruitier light wines than before.

The 'wine bazaar'

The result of all this exporting of wine is that Valencia is the greatest 'wine bazaar' in Spain. An extraordinary array of goods is prepared for shipment in the wineries: great black demijohns of strong red wine for West Africa; rustic-looking wicker-covered flasks for Germany; blue barrels of wine concentrate for Japan; and pallets of canned Sangria (a spiced and sweetened wine drink) for the United States. It is an extraordinary sight and not one to appeal to the wine snob. But it cannot disguise that the region produces some of the best-value, everyday wines in Spain and some that are very much better than that. Not quite up to the standards of the northern regions perhaps. But interesting and well worth tasting.

The great wine companies

The largest of these companies is the giant VINIVAL in El Grao. Its extraordinary modern winery, nicknamed the 'cathedral' by some, and less flattering names by others, can be seen from the A7 as one approaches the city. Its brown brick exterior looks like a collection of upturned cigar tubes (see page 124).

Inside, however, the equipment is all modern, while in a separate building, two fast bottling lines are constantly in action, demonstrating just what extraordinary quantities of wine are involved in this modernized industry.

Also in El Grao are the two Swiss-owned companies, Bodegas Schenk and Augusto Egli. Both are housed in their original buildings, although these have now been thoroughly modernized. And both produce a wide range of wines and are a hive of activity.

As there is little room for expansion in El Grao, the last great wine firm of Valencia, Vicente Gandía Pla, has long since moved to the town of Chiva, the first stop of our tour of the Levante interior.

Vicente Gandía Pla's modern winery in Chiva, outside Valencia, is among the most advanced in the country. This construction would be quite at home in the Napa Valley of California.

VALENCIA (cont.)
VINIVAL Av. Novelista Blasco Ibañez 2, 46120 Alboraya, (Valencia). Tel: 371 86 11. Fax: 372 90 99. (Juan Antonio Mompó). Mon-Fri 0900-1400. Closed Aug. E. ☎

The Wine Country of Valencia

CHIVA
Vicente Gandía Pla Ctra.
Cheste a Godelleta s/n,
46370 Chiva, (Valencia). Tel:
252 24 43. Fax: 252 05 67.
(Silvia Gandía). Open all week
by previous appointment (at
least four days beforehand).
Closed Aug. E.F.TF.WS. ☎

BUNOL
RECOMMENDED RESTAURANT
Venta de l'Home Ctra.
Valencia-Madrid Km.45. Tel:
250 35 15. Old coach house.

From Valencia, take the busy N111 in
the direction of Chiva. This route
leads through extensive orange groves
before starting the slow climb to the
central plateau of Spain. Here you
are deep in the D.O. Valencia, a
confusing region with a myriad of
microclimates and grape varieties.

Although some reds and *rosados* are
made here, this is primarily white
wine country, with its production
based on the Merseguera – not the
best variety in Spain, but capable of
producing light and fresh wines when
well vinified. Gandía Pla produces
good examples of these and above-
average reds and *rosados* in its brand
new, purpose-built winery just off the
main road.

Then it is on up the N111 to the
Venta de l'Home restaurant, which
sits on a bend of the road near the
small town of Buñol. This is an old

coach house dating back to the 18th
century and its regional cuisine
makes it an ideal place to stop at
lunchtime.

The wine country
Buñol is also close to the border
between the Denomination of
Valencia and that of Utiel-Requena,
a border marked by the deep furrow
of the Cabriel river. As most of the
wine from both Denominations is
marketed by the big firms of
Valencia, the link between them is
strong. Furthermore, their wines are
complementary: while most of
Valencia's production is of white, that
of Utiel-Requena is of red and *rosado*
as the region is dominated by the
Bobal, a variety that produces very
acceptable young wines of both
colours. Its main weakness, however,
is that its wines do not age well. The
local *Consejo*, therefore, has been
actively encouraging the planting of
varieties with greater staying power
and the hectorage of Cencibel, in
particular, is increasing. The
Denomination also produces Cava
sparkling wines.

The co-operatives
The region's production is dominated
by the co-operatives, the most typical
being those of the towns of Utiel and
Requena themselves. Both Augusto
Egli and, more recently, Gandía Pla
have vineyards in the region,
however, and if you wish to visit the
second, ask at the winery in Chiva.

Utiel-Requena
Lying at an altitude of 800m (2600 ft)
Utiel-Requena is close to the borders
of both La Mancha and Aragon.
This proximity to the old kingdom of
the north becomes apparent as you

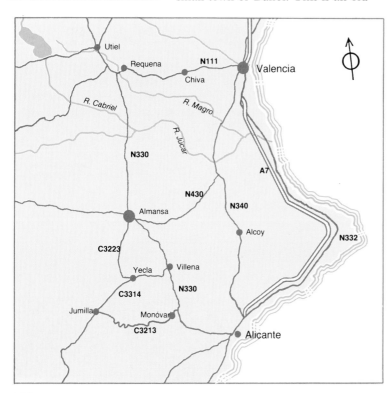

drive from Requena to Almansa along the narrow N330, which leads through a landscape of fir trees and orchards. Slowly the ochre soil that is so dominant as far south as the province of Teruel begins to blend with the pale yellow of the southern Levante. Then the road plunges down into the valley formed by the Embalse de Embarcaderos.

This is a place of great natural beauty with the walls of the valley revealing intermingled layers of ochre and yellow rock and earth. Unfortunately it is also here that the Spanish government decided to build a huge nuclear power station, complete with a dam and maze of access roads.

Almansa

Almansa is at the eastern end of the province of Albacete where La Mancha meets the Levante. But its wines are more Levantine in character, made from the Monastrell rather than the Cencibel and the small amount of white it produces is mostly from the Merseguera.

This is a small Denomination that sells most of its wine in bulk. The family-owned Bodegas Piqueras, however, produces good examples of what the region is capable of, some light, pleasant whites and rosés and more robust reds including some oak-aged *reservas*.

ALMANSA
Bodegas Piqueras
Juan Ramón Jimenez 3, Almansa, (Albacete).
Tel: 341 482. Fax: 345 480. (Juan Pablo Bonete). Mon-Fri 0900-1300, 1600-1900.
E.TF.WS.

RECOMMENDED RESTAURANT

Mesón del Pincelín
Las Norisas 10. Tel: 34 00 07. In the town centre with splendid, hearty food.

Almansa's medieval fortress, perched on its rocky mound, is a local landmark.

The Levantine Interior

An ancient wine press forms a doorway at Bodegas Asencio Carcelén in Jumilla. Carcelén is one of the most traditional wine companies in the Denomination, but is unfortunately not open to the public.

YECLA
Bodegas Castaño
Ctra. de Fuentealamo 3, Yecla, (Murcia). Tel: 79 11 15. Fax: 79 19 00. (Daniel Castaño). Mon-Fri 0830-1330, 1530-1800. E.TF.WS. ☎

Yecla

After a visit to the old castle, take the C3223 to Yecla, centre of the Denomination of that name. This is a dusty, unattractive town with a constant flow of trucks, and the Denomination itself is in decline – partly because of the fall in demand for the bulk wines which were its life-blood, and partly because of a lack of investment. It does, however, have one very good producer, Bodegas Castaño, which, fired by the enthusiasm of its enologist, is producing some attractive wines under the Las Gruesas label.

Here the traditional style of heavy, muscle-bound reds and rosés bulging with extract and tannin, and dull, alcoholic whites has been discarded in favour of lighter wines with greater acidity and fruitiness. The winery is to the west of the town and worth visiting. The C3314 then leads on to Jumilla.

Jumilla wines

This is an altogether more agreeable town, leafier and quieter and it was once the centre of a thriving wine industry. Then, in the late 1980s, the phylloxera finally caught up with it – a century after it hit other parts of Spain. Sales, which stood at over 67 million litres (about 16 million gallons) in 1989, fell to just under 29 million litres (6-7 million gallons) in 1993.

This destruction, however, has given the Denomination the opportunity to start again. Much of the wine that it used to produce was similar to Yecla's, making it equally dependent on the bulk market. The shock of the past few years, however, has made its wine makers think again about the style of wine that they want to produce.

Now the vineyards are being replanted, outside investment has been attracted and the Monastrell has proved to be capable of producing some good red wines. These are mostly young *tintos jovenes* but there are also some powerful, long lasting *crianzas* and *reservas* beginning to emerge from the region. And they are doing so at prices that are undoubtedly good value.

The town of Jumilla

There are several co-operatives in the town and some privately-owned companies. The most picturesque of these, Asencio Carcelén founded in the 19th century, is unfortunately not open to the public. For a tasting and an understanding of how the Denomination works, therefore, you have to go to the huge Señorio del Condestable.

This is owned by the largest wine company in Spain, Bodegas y Bebidas, which has invested heavily in the winery. Its wines, therefore, are very much in the 'modern' style and the range is comprehensive.

Monóvar

The final stop in our tour of the Levantine interior is the town of Monóvar in the Denomination of Alicante which is approached along the C3213 from Jumilla.

This is the second largest of the region's wine towns and is the birthplace of the author Azorín, whose house is now a museum – as well as the home of the Denomination's leading wine firm – and can be visited by appointment with the *Ayuntamiento* or town hall.

Alicante's wine industry used to be very similar to that of Jumilla and Yecla. From being primarily a bulk wine producer, however, it is now becoming more adventurous and more interested in producing wines that people outside the region want to drink.

Leading this development is the family-owned firm of Salvador Poveda. It also produces the best example of the region's main speciality, the oak aged and fortified Fondillón. The wine's long ageing, during which some 50 per cent is said to evaporate, gives it a light copper colour and immense smoothness and intensity. An appropriate climax to what can be a hot but always interesting tour of the Levantine interior.

Further travel

For those restricting themselves to a tour of the Levante, the C3213 meets the larger N330 just after Monóvar, and this leads directly to Alicante. After the heat and heavy wines of the interior, this city, with its beaches, its wonderful restaurants and its thriving night life, is the perfect place to recuperate.

Those looking for further exertions are advised to go southwards to Murcia and then take the N340 and the N342 (not the most exciting of drives) to the fabulous city of Granada, a gateway to the great fortified wine regions of Andalusia.

From there a circular route takes in Málaga, Jerez (either along the coast road or through Ronda), and Córdoba, with its neighbouring region of Montilla. Then the route outlined in the earlier chapters of this book can be followed in reverse, through the two Castilles and Madrid to the Rioja, and Navarra, ending up either at Bilbao or at the French border at the western end of the Pyrenees.

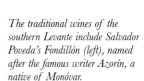

The traditional wines of the southern Levante include Salvador Poveda's Fondillón (left), named after the famous writer Azorín, a native of Monóvar.

JUMILLA
Señorio del Condestable
Av. Reyes Catolicos s/n, 30520 Jumilla, (Murcia). Tel: 78 10 11. Fax: 78 11 00. (Alberto Perez). Mon-Fri 0900-1400. E.TP.WS. ☎

RECOMMENDED RESTAURANT
Casa Sebastián Av. Levante 6. Tel: 78 01 94. Next to the Abastos market.

MONOVAR
Salvador Poveda
Benjamín Palencia 19, 03640 Monóvar, (Alicante). Tel: 696 01 80. Fax: 547 33 89. (Rafael Poveda). Mon-Fri 0700-1500. E.F.TF.WS.

RECOMMENDED RESTAURANT
Xiri Parque la Alameda s/n. Tel: 547 29 10.

MURCIA

RECOMMENDED RESTAURANT
El Rincón de Pepe Clle. Apóstoles 34, 30001 Murcia. Tel: 21 22 39. Typical southern Levantine cuisine.

Food and Festivals of the Levante

LEVANTINE CUISINE

The most famous dish of the Levante is the paella. Valencia is Spain's greatest rice producer, growing large quantities of the top-quality, short-grained variety in the flat, swampy area around Lake Albufera to the south of the city. The irrigation system here was first built by the Moors. Rice has been the staple diet of the coastal area for centuries, and its people have traditionally added to it what they could afford: fish, snails and vegetables to begin with and, in more recent, prosperous years, more expensive ingredients such as chicken, beef and shellfish.

Today, there are countless different types of paella, some of which are wonderfully elaborate, most of them including chicken and shellfish, and coloured with golden saffron.

In the inland areas of Almansa, Utiel-Requena, Jumilla and Yecla, the cuisine is very different. Fish and rice disappear from the menu and are replaced by beans, potatoes and small game, cooked in *ollas* or stews and flavoured with mountain herbs such as thyme and rosemary. The best example is the splendid *Gazpacho Manchego* or *Alicantino*, a true shepherd's dish, hearty, filling and good protection against the colder climate of the interior.

FOOD SPECIALITIES

Doradas a la Sal Fish baked encased in coarse sea salt to keep it moist. Many different kinds of fish are used, but the most popular is the *dorada*.
Gazpacho Alicantino or *Manchego* In contrast to the southern cold soup, this is a strong stew. Its ingredients vary but are usually small game such as partridge and rabbit. In some versions a *torta*, a hard biscuit made with flour and water, is broken up

into pieces to absorb the juices; in others the stew is poured over it and, after the meal, the underside is spread with honey as a dessert.
Paella The classic version of this dish combines rice with chicken, beef, vegetables (green beans, peppers and tomatoes), shellfish (mussels, prawns) and squid and snails. A fisherman's version is the *Paella de Mariscos* with only shellfish, while an interesting alternative is the *Paella de Caza* with small game and often snails.

FESTIVALS

The Levante has some spectacular fiestas but not all are directly related to wine. Virtually every wine town in the region, of course, celebrates the coming of the *vendimia*, when the first must is blessed in the central square, but none of these festivities is particularly remarkable or unique. The best known are those of Requena at the end of August/beginning of September, and of Jumilla about a week earlier.

There are, however, two uniquely Levantine festivals in early spring. These festivals will appeal to those who enjoy spectacular shows and historic celebrations, as well as to the traveller who likes to drink wine and have fun during a great occasion.

The first is the *Fallas*, which takes place in the city of Valencia during the week leading up to St Joseph's Day on 19 March. The usual religious processions and ritual bullfights take place, but they culminate in a blazing orgy of bonfires, when life-size wax figures, some of which have taken six months or more to build, are set alight.

The second other great Levantine celebration is the series of 'Moors and Christians' festivals which take place in many towns. The most famous is in the small town of Alcoy near Villena, in April. The townspeople dress up in Moorish and Christian costumes and re-enact the battles that took place in the region during the period of the Reconquest. Both of these spectacles are unique.

During the Fallas, *massive firework displays and bonfires light up the night sky above the city of Valencia.*

The Islands – the Balearics and Canaries

THE BALEARICS

MALLORCA

BINISSALEM
Bodegas José L. Ferrer.
Franja Roja Clle.
Conquistador 103 C.P.
07350 Binissalem,
(Mallorca). Tel: 51 10 50.
Fax: 87 00 84. (José Luis
and Sebastian Roses
Ferrer). Mon-Fri 0800-
1900, Sat 1000-1400.
E.TP.WS. ☎

**PALMA DE
MALLORCA**

RECOMMENDED RESTAURANT
Koldo Royo Paseo
Maritimo 3. Tel: 73 24 35.
For excellent local food.

RECOMMENDED WINE SHOP
Casa Llofriu San Nicolas
22. For an excellent
selection of local wines.

THE CANARIES

LAS PALMAS

RECOMMENDED WINE SHOP
**El Gabinete
Gastronomico** Torres 18.
Good selection of Canaries
wines. Wine tastings. Also
local cigars.

TENERIFE

RECOMMENDED WINE SHOP
Caribbean Center
Viera y Clavijo s/n. Good
selection of Canaries
wines.

Neither the Balearics, off the coast of Catalonia, nor the Canaries, near the coast of north-west Africa, produce large quantities of wine today. Despite their long viticultural traditions – wine has been made in the Balearics since the second century B.C. and Shakespeare refers to 'Canary Sack' – both industries are mere shadows of what they once were.

The reasons are twofold: on both island groups there is enormous pressure from the tourist industry; and, in the Canaries, viticultural conditions are unbelievably harsh.

Nevertheless both industries are going through something of a renaissance. In the early 1990s one Denomination was set up in Mallorca and seven more on different islands of the Canaries. This development has encouraged a number of go-ahead wine companies to play to their strengths and produce well-vinified wines from their unique grape varieties.

The Balearics

The Denomination of Binissalem is located in the 'high zone' of Mallorca just above Palma. It protects a mere 312 hectares (770 acres) of vineyard, planted primarily with the autochthonous Manto Negro, Callet and Moll, with pockets of mainland varieties such as the Tempranillo, Monastrell, Macabeo and Parellada. Some foreign varieties such as the Chardonnay and the Cabernet Sauvignon have also been planted.

Production is in the hands of a few, family-owned companies that grow and crush their own grapes. Red wine, which must have at least 50 per cent Manto Negro to qualify for the Binissalem back-label, predominates, and some of it is aged in barrel to produce excellent mature wines.

While on holiday, therefore, it is well worth taking a day excursion to the region. Binissalem is a charming little town and is home to Bodegas José Ferrer, which produces a good range of wines from autochthonous varieties and gives the visitor a good idea of what the Denomination is capable of.

The Canaries

The Canaries now has seven D.O.s scattered across its islands. Some of these, however, are tiny: the Denomination of La Palma, for example, covers no more than 600 hectares (1500 acres); that of Valle de la Orotava about 1000 hectares (2500 acres).

With hot winds blowing from the Sahara, volcanic terrain and little to no rainfall, viticulture here is very difficult indeed, and the vines survive on the dew which is absorbed by the porous volcanic stone. In Lanzarote, each vine has to be planted in a pit sometimes up to three metres (10ft) deep, or is surrounded by a stone wall to protect it from the wind. This technique makes viticulture expensive. Add high transport costs, and it is not surprising that very little wine from the Canaries is ever seen outside the islands.

Here too there are some unique and interesting grape varieties planted. Shakespeare's Sack was made from the perfumed Malvasia and there is still plenty of it around producing the classic, amber-coloured, wood-aged sweet wines. But other varieties, such as the Listan (red and white) are now being vinified to make lighter, more 'modern' wines.

Reference Section

GLOSSARY OF FOOD AND WINE TERMS

Aguardiente A fiery transparent spirit distilled from wine.
Ajo Garlic.
Albariza The white soil of Jerez, with a high limestone content.
Alcachofa Artichoke.
Allioli A popular sauce in Catalonia made from garlic and olive oil.
Amontillado A type of sherry or Montilla.
Arroz Rice.
Asado A roast.
Asador A restaurant that specializes in roasted meats.

Bacalao Cod.
Barrica The classic 225-litre oak barrel, usually made of oak.
Bodega A winery or wine cellar.
Bodeguero The owner or manager of a bodega.
Brut or **Brut nature** A dry Cava.
Butifarra Type of sausage particularly popular in Catalonia and the Balearics.

Cachelada A stew.
Caldereta A stew, or the pot it is cooked in.
Callos Tripe.
Capataz A master taster in Jerez.
Cava A sparkling wine made by the *Método Clásico* or *Méthode Champenoise*. The term comes from the word *cava*, a cellar.
Chilindrón A type of sauce made from peppers, tomatoes and garlic, popular in Aragon, Navarra and the Rioja.
Chorizo A spicy sausage not unlike the French *saucisson*.
Chuleta A chop. A **chuletón** is larger.
Clarete A light red wine usually made with a mixture of red and white grapes.
Cochinillo Sucking pig.
Codorniz Quail.
Conejo Rabbit.
Consejo Regulador The Regulating Council of a Denomination of Origin, which enforces strict standards of quality and authenticity.
Copita The traditional slender sherry glass, tapered in towards the mouth.
Cordero Lamb.
Cosecha Vintage.
Coupage A blend of wines or grape varieties.

Cream A type of sherry or Montilla.
Criadera An oak butt used in the *solera* system.
Crianza A wine that has been aged in oak barrels.

Degüelle The disgorging process used for sparkling wines.
Dorada A type of fish popular in the Levante.
Dorado A fortified golden wine made in Rueda.
Dulce Sweet. Also used for a sweet type of Cava.

Estofado A stew.

Fino A type of dry sherry or Montilla.
Flor A layer of yeasts formed inside the butt of sherry or Montilla on the surface of the wine.
Fondillón A rare matured wine made in the southern Levante.

Garnatxa d'Emporda A sweet dessert wine made in the Ampurdán.
Gazpacho In Andalusia this is a cold vegetable soup; in the Levante and La Mancha it is a hearty stew.
Generoso A fortified *apéritif* or dessert wine.
Gran Reserva A wine matured for many years in barrel and bottle.
Granvas A sparkling wine made by the *Cuvé Clos* method.

Habas Broad beans.
Horno (de asar) An oven.

Jamón Ham.
Judias Beans: *judias blancas* are haricot beans; *judias negras* are runner beans.

Lágrima A sweet wine made from the free-run must of the grapes.
Licor de Tiraje A sweet wine added to sparkling wines in different measures to achieve different levels of sweetness.

Manzanilla A very dry sherry made in Sanlúcar de Barrameda.
Masía A country house or winery in Catalonia.
Méthode champenoise The superior method of making sparkling wines. The second fermentation takes place within the bottle, as opposed to tanks.

Migas Breadcrumbs or flour fried in olive oil.
Morcilla A black sausage, akin to black pudding.
Moscatel A sweet dessert wine made from the Moscatel grape.
Must Grape juice before fermentation.

Négociant Wine broker.

Olla A stew pot.
Oloroso A type of sherry or Montilla.

Paella The famous dish from the Levante made with meat, fish, vegetables and rice.
Pale Cream A type of sherry or Montilla.
Pálido Pale. Also used for a fortified wine from Rueda.
Palo Cortado A rare type of sherry.
Parrillada A grill popular in Catalonia.
Patatas Potatoes.
Pato Duck.
Perdiz Partridge.
Pétillant Slightly sparkling or effervescent.
Phylloxera A louse that attacks and destroys the roots of the vine. The European industry has defeated it by grafting its stock on to resistant American rootstock.
Picada A sauce made with saffron, garlic, nuts, parsley and cinnamon.
Pimiento Pepper.
Pinchito A small kebab usually served as a tapa.

Rancio An old white wine that has been matured and allowed to oxidize in barrel.
Rape Hake.
Removido The turning process used for sparkling wine. The bottles are gradually turned upside down so that the sediment settles on the cork, prior to its removal by *degüelle*.
Reserva A wine that has been matured in barrel and bottle.
Revuelto de Setas A mushroom omelette.
Romesco A type of sauce made with garlic, tomatoes, peppers, bread and almonds, very popular in Catalonia.
Rosado Rosé wine.
Rovellón A type of wild mushroom found in Catalonia.

Samfaina A sauce made with aubergines, tomatoes, onions, and courgettes.

Sangría A drink made with wine, brandy and fruit.

Seco Dry. Also used to describe a dryish sort of Cava.

Sofrito A sauce of sautéed onions, tomatoes, peppers and garlic in olive oil.

Solera system The system used in the production of sherry, Montilla and Malaga. The *solera* is the butt of wine at ground level; the upper butts are known as *criaderas*.

Tannin A substance in the grape pips and stalks which gives the wine its backbone and staying power, enabling it to last longer.

Tapas Small dishes or appetizers served with drinks at a bar.

Ternera Veal.

Tinaja Large earthenware amphora-shaped containers in which wine is stored.

Torta A hard flour biscuit served with Gazpacho Manchego.

Tortilla An omelette.

Trucha Trout.

Varietal Wine made from a single grape variety.

Vendimia Grape harvest.

Vendimiador Grape picker.

Venencia A small thin silver cup attached to a whalebone; used by the *venenciador* to extract samples from the sherry butts and pour them into glasses.

Vi de l'any A Catalan wine, particularly from the Ampurdán, released just a few months after fermentation.

Vino Wine.

Vino de aguja 'Needle' wine, a wine with a slight *pétillance*.

Vino de l'año A wine intended to be consumed within a year of the harvest.

Vino del cosechero A wine produced by a small grape farmer, usually sold by the jug or demijohn.

Zarzuela A fish stew, particularly popular in Catalonia.

Zurracapote A wine mixed with fruit and cinnamon.

PRINCIPAL GRAPE VARIETIES

The following varieties are the principal grapes used in Spain:

Airén (white). The principal variety of Castilla La Mancha, the Airén can produce pleasant, light and fruity young whites which are often rather neutral.

Albariño (white). Planted mostly in Galicia and producing wines with good acidity balanced with delicate, complex and often honeyed fruitiness. Tends to be rather low in aromas.

Bobal (black). A hardy vine planted mostly in the Levante. Its wines tend to oxidize quickly, but it can produce good *rosados*.

Cabernet Sauvignon (black). One of the world's great travellers, and now one of the most popular imported 'noble' varieties in Spain, planted increasingly in Navarra and Catalonia. South of the Pyrenees it produces enormous wines that are packed with colour, fruit and tannin and thus are often blended with softer grape varieties.

Cariñena (black). Also known as the Mazuelo, and planted in parts of Aragon and Catalonia with smaller pockets in the Rioja. It produces wines that are deep in colour, dry and with a high degree of alcohol and extract.

Cencibel. See Tempranillo.

Chardonnay (white). Another favourite import. In Spain it can produce some almost overpoweringly fruity and intense wines, but it is usually used in blends, to add touches of finesse and depth to both still wines and Cavas.

Garnacha (black). An indigenous Spanish variety known in France as the Grenache, this is now the most widely planted black variety in Spain, particularly in Navarra, the Rioja and Aragon. When well vinified, it produces excellent, open and very fruity wines, so it is ideal for young reds and rosés. Its biggest weakness is its lack of tannin and staying power.

Graciano (black). Planted in small parcels in the Rioja Alta, it produces wines with good staying power, delicate aroma and flavour. Unfortunately, it is usually blended, but it can make a good blend into a really great one.

Macabeo. See Viura.

Malvasía (white). Planted in increasingly small parcels in the Rioja, Navarra and the Canaries. It produces wines of character, with good body and aroma.

Mazuelo. See Cariñena.

Merseguera (white). Planted widely in the Levante, particularly Valencia. Its pale wines can be fresh and fruity, but they tend to lack charm.

Monastrell (black). Again, a favourite variety in the Levante particularly in the southern part of the region, where it produces wines that are big in body, dry, high in alcohol, and long lasting.

Palomino (white). The great variety of Jerez, the Palomino produces wines which lack character and are low in sugar and acidity. It is the *solera* system that transforms the unremarkable wines into excellent sherries.

Parellada (white). This is the best white variety in Catalonia, and particularly the Penedès, where it produces wines of great freshness and crispness, with good fruit and aroma.

Pedro Ximénez (white). Widely planted in Montilla, and used in Jerez to make sweetening wines. It produces fairly neutral wines with a high level of alcohol (not surprisingly, considering the southern sun). Again, it is the *solera* system that transforms the wine.

Tempranillo (black). Also known as the Ull de Llebre in Catalonia, and as the Cencibel in New Castile and the Levante. The Tinto Fino of Old Castile is a close variant. Usually considered to be the best native black variety in Spain, it is planted in increasing quantities all over the country. In the Rioja and Navarra it produces wines with good aroma, fruit and colour, and a moderate level of alcohol – qualities that are enhanced further south in New Castile, where the alcohol level can reach 14 to 15 per cent. It blends well with the Garnacha, which adds extra fruit and alcohol; the Tempranillo provides the elegance and finesse.

Tinto Fino. See Tempranillo.

Ull de Llebre. See Tempranillo.

Verdejo (white). A native of Old Castile, increasingly planted in Rueda. Verdejo is capable of producing wines of elegance, crisp, well-balanced, fruity and characterful.

Viura (white). Also known as the Macabeo, and planted in the Rioja, Navarra, Catalonia and the Levante. Its wines are crisp, fruity and with good aroma, but they often lack character.

Xarel.lo (white). The third variety of the Penedès, this grape produces wines that can be coarse, but they have body, acidity and a relatively high level of alcohol.

SPANISH VINTAGES

Spain has more hectares under vine than any other country in Europe, and the grapes are grown in climatic conditions that vary considerably: the conditions in Jerez, for example, could not be more different than those in, say, the Ribera del Duero.

It is therefore always difficult to generalize about Spain's vintages.

In general, however, a distinction may be made between those regions that are influenced by the Mediterranean, and those in the southern part of the country (namely Catalonia, New Castile, the Levante and Andalusia), and those that are influenced by the Atlantic (namely Navarra, the Rioja, Old Castile and Galicia). In the former regions the climate is generally consistent, and produces crops that vary little in quality or quantity, except in very exceptional years when late frosts, hailstorms and mildew can reduce yields. In recent years, namely 1994 and 1995, yields were also affected by

a severe drought across the country. In the Atlantic regions, the climate is less consistent, and both the quality and the quantity of the *vendimias* vary considerably.

It must also be noted that, traditionally, Spanish red wines are only released when they are ready for drinking, in contrast to, for example, Bordeaux or Burgundy. And again in contrast to the wines of these two great French regions, Spanish wines tend to reach a plateau comparatively early, and then to stay on it for several years.

The following vintage chart for Spain's four leading quality regions has been compiled from the reports of the *Consejos Reguladores*, which classify their vintages from 'excellent' to 'poor' (though the latter category is rarely used). As most Spanish white wines are now made to drink early, this chart is limited to red wines only.

Note: this is a general guide; unfortunately there can always be exceptions.

	Rioja	Navarra	Penedès	Ribera del Duero	Symbols
1978	VG	VG	E	G	**E** excellent
1979	A	A	A	VG	**VG** very good
1980	G	A	VG	G	**G** good
1981	VG	E	VG	VG	**A** average
1982	E	E	VG	E	**P** poor.
1983	G	VG	G	G	
1984	A	VG	VG	A	Older vintages to look
1985	G	G	VG	G	out for (although they
1986	G	G	G	G	are increasingly hard to
1987	VG	VG	E	A/G	find, even in Spain)
1988	G	VG	G	A/P	include the following:
1989	A/G	E	A	VG	1973 (Navarra and
1990	G	G	G	VG	Ribera del Duero); 1970
1991	VG	G	VG	VG	(all regions);1969
1992	G	G	G	G	(Penedès); 1968 (all
1993	G	VG	VG	A	regions); 1966 (Penedès);
1994	E	VG	G	VG	1964 (all regions; this
1995	E	E	G	E	year amounts to a
					legend in the Rioja).

Further Information

METRIC EQUIVALENTS		
Kilometres		**Miles**
1.61	1	0.62
3.22	2	1.24
4.83	3	1.86
6.44	4	2.49
8.05	5	3.11
9.66	6	3.73
11.27	7	4.35
12.88	8	5.59
14.48	9	5.59
64.37	10	6.21
80.47	50	31.07
96.56	60	37.28
112.65	70	43.50
128.75	80	49.71
144.84	90	55.92
160.93	100	62.14
Hectares		**Acres**
0.41	1	2.47
0.81	2	4.94
1.21	3	7.41
1.62	4	9.88
2.02	5	12.36
2.43	6	14.83
2.83	7	17.30
3.24	8	19.77
3.64	9	22.24
4.05	10	24.71
8.09	20	49.42
12.14	30	74.13
16.19	40	98.84
20.23	50	123.56
24.28	60	148.26
28.33	70	172.97
32.37	80	197.68
36.42	90	222.40
40.47	100	247.11

Wines from Spain

This is a wine information and promotion bureau, and can be very helpful for advice, leaflets, addresses and general information:
(U.K.) 66 Chiltern Street, London W1M 2LS. Tel: 0171-486 0101. Fax: 0171-487 5586.
(U.S.A.) 405 Lexington Avenue, New York, N.Y. 10174-0331. Tel: (212) 661 4959. Fax: (212) 972 2494.

Consejos Reguladores

Alternatively, when you are in Spain, the *Consejos Reguladores* for each Denomination of Origin can prove helpful, and they also provide information leaflets. It must be stressed, however, that these organizations are generally very busy, and they do not often have English speakers on their staff:

Alella Masía Musen Municipal Can Magarola, 08328 Alella, (Barcelona). Tel: (93) 540 02 16. Fax: 540 03 28.
Alicante Profesor Manuel Sala 2, 03003 Alicante. Tel: (96) 590 06 13. Fax: 590 06 88.
Almansa Mendez Nuñez 7, 02640 Almansa, (Albacete). Tel: (967) 34 02 58. Fax: 34 02 58.
Ampurdán-Costa Brava Blanc 10-11, 17600 Figueres, (Girona). Tel: (972) 50 75 13. Fax: 51 00 58.
Campo de Borja Av. San Andrés 6, 50570 Ainzón, (Zaragoza). Tel: (976) 85 21 22. Fax: 86 88 06.
Cariñena Camino de la Platera 7, 50400 Cariñena, (Zaragoza). Tel: (976) 62 06 94. Fax: 62 11 07.
Cava Av. Tarragona 24, 08720 Vilafranca del Penedès, (Barcelona). Tel: (93) 890 31 04. Fax: 890 15 67.
Costers del Segre Camp de Marte 35, 25004 Lerida. Tel: (973) 24 66 50. Fax: 24 89 29.
Jumilla San Roque 15, 30520 Jumilla, (Murcia). Tel: (968) 78 17 61. Fax: 78 19 00.
La Mancha Calle Canalejas 37, Apartado 194, 13600 Alcázar de San Juan, (Ciudad Real). Tel: (926) 54 15 23. Fax: 54 65 39.
Málaga Fernando Camino 2-33, 29016 Málaga. Tel: (952) 22 79 90. Fax: 22 79 90.
Montilla Ronda de los Tejares 24-5, 14001 Córdoba. Tel: (957) 47 54 84. Fax: 47 75 19.
Navarra Conde Oliveta 2 izq., Apartado 399, 31002 Pamplona, (Navarra). Tel: (948) 22 78 52. Fax: 21 21 01.
Penedès Amalia Soler 27, 08720 Vilafranca del Penedès, (Barcelona). Tel: (93) 890 48 11. Fax: 890 47 54.
Priorat Paseo Sunyer s/n, 43202 Reus, (Tarragona). Tel: (977) 31 20 32. Fax: 33 16 55.
Rías Baixas Cabanas-Salcedo, 36143 Salcedo, (Pontevedra). Tel: (986) 85 48 50. Fax: 86 45 46.
Ribeiro Bajada de Oliveira s/n, 32400 Ribadavia, (Orense). Tel: (988) 47 10 15. Fax: 47 13 52.
Ribera del Duero Hospital s/n, 09300 Roa de Duero, (Burgos). Tel: (947) 54 12 21. Fax: 54 11 16.
Rioja Jorge Vigón 51, 26003 Logroño, (La Rioja). Tel: (941) 24 11 99. Fax: 25 35 02.
Rueda Real 8, 47490 Rueda, (Valladolid). Tel: (983) 86 82 48. Fax: 86 82 48.
Sherry Av. Alvaro Domecq 2, 11405 Jerez de la Frontera (Cádiz). Tel: (956) 33 20 50. Fax: 33 89 08.
Somontano Av. Navarra 1, 22300 Barbastro, (Huesca). Tel: (976) 31 30 31. Fax: 31 30 31.

Terra Alta Av. Cataluña 5, 43780 Gandesa, (Tarragona). Tel: (977) 42 01 46. Fax: 42 06 35.
Toro Plaza España 7,49800 Toro, (Zamora).Tel: (980) 69 03 35. Fax: 69 03 35.
Utiel-Requena Sevilla 12, 46300 Utiel, (Valencia). Tel: (96) 217 10 62. Fax: 217 21 85.
Valdepeñas Clle. Constitución 19, 1330 Valdepeñas (Ciudad Real). Tel: (926) 32 27 88.Fax: 32 10 54.
Valencia Quart 22, 46001 Valencia. Tel: (96) 391 00 96. Fax: 391 00 29.
Yecla Corredera 14, 30510 Yecla, (Murcia). Tel: (968) 79 23 52. Fax: 79 23 52.

Tourist offices
Spain receives some 50 million foreign tourists each year (most of whom stay in the coastal resorts) and there are tourist offices in most of its major towns. These can be useful for local information, and they will usually be able to provide the traveller with a great variety of useful information such as town maps, lists of local hotels and Paradors, youth hostels, and so forth. If you are based in the U.K. or U.S.A., the Spanish Tourist Office can provide the addresses of local tourist offices in Spain:

The Spanish National Tourist Office
(U.K.) Metro House, 57/58 St James's St, London SW1A 1LD. Tel: (0171) 499 1169. Fax: 629 4257.
(U.S.A.) 666 Fifth Avenue, New York, N.Y. 10103. Tel: (212) 265 8822. Fax: (212) 265 8864.

Otherwise, for the same information, there is a large central office in Madrid:
Oficina Nacional de Turismo Duque de Medinacinali 2, Madrid. Tel: (91) 429 59 51/429 44 87. Fax: (91) 429 09 09.

Consulates
Consulate addresses can be found in the local telephone director, listed under the heading 'Consulado de la Gran Bretaña' or 'Consulado del Reino Unido' (Great Britain or the United Kingdom), or 'Consulado de los Estados Unidos' (United States). Otherwise, the national or local tourist offices should be able to provide them.

Hotels and Paradors
See page 14.

Camping and caravans
Though perfectly legal, rough camping or the parking of caravans outside recognized sites is frowned upon by the authorities, and can be dangerous. In fact, Spain has numerous camping sites (over 350) and, although the great majority are to be found along the coast, some of them are in wonderful inland locations. For a list of sites and further information or advice, either contact the local Tourist Office, or:
International Camping Federation (I.Z.V.) Edificio España, Plaza de España, Madrid. Tel: (91) 242 10 89. It is perhaps worth repeating that some of the routes described in the course of this book (particularly the tour of the Priorat and the interior of Levante) are not recommended for caravan travel.

METRIC EQUIVALENTS		
Litres		**Imperial Gallons**
4.55	1	0.22
9.09	2	0.44
13.64	3	0.66
18.18	4	0.88
22.73	5	1.10
27.28	6	1.32
31.82	7	1.54
36.37	8	1.76
40.91	9	1.98
45.46	10	2.20
90.92	20	4.40
136.38	30	6.60
181.84	40	8.80
227.30	50	11.00
272.76	60	13.20
318.22	70	15.40
363.68	80	17.60
409.14	90	19.80
454.60	100	22.00
Litres		**U.S.Gallons**
3.79	1	0.26
7.57	2	0.53
11.36	3	0.79
15.14	4	1.06
18.93	5	1.32
22.71	6	1.59
26.50	7	1.85
30.28	8	2.11
34.07	9	2.38
37.85	10	2.64
75.71	20	5.28
113.56	30	7.92
151.41	40	10.56
189.27	50	13.21
227.12	60	15.85
264.97	70	18.49
302.82	80	21.13
340.68	90	23.78
378.53	100	26.42

Public holidays

Virtually every town and city in Spain celebrates the feast day of its patron saint and, if this day happens to be one day away from the weekend, the day in between also becomes a holiday (known as a *puente* or bridge). Most of the bodegas will close, so it is very important to get information on local holidays from the local Tourist Office as soon as you can. In addition, there are the following national holidays:

January 1 (New Year)
January 6 (Epiphany)
March 19 (St Joseph)
End March/early April Maundy Thursday, Good Friday, Easter Monday (Easter usually amounts to an extended holiday)
May 1 (Labour Day)
Corpus Christi (the second Thursday after Whitsun)
July 25 (St James the Apostle)
August 15 (Assumption)
October 12 (Our Lady of El Pilar)
November 1 (All Saints' Day)
December 8 (Immaculate Conception)
December 25 (Christmas and New Year tend to become an extended holiday)

Using the telephone in Spain

Public telephones are preferable to those in hotel rooms, which are very expensive to use. The public telephones also give clear pictorial instructions for their use.

Each Spanish province has its code number (as listed). To phone a number in another province you must dial 9 and then the appropriate provincial code. (For example, to phone a number in the province of Barcelona when you are outside the province, dial 93 [prefix and code], followed by the number.) You don't need the code if you are phoning a number within the same province.

Sample letter to a bodega owner

[Sender's name, address, telephone and/or fax number, and date]

Muy Señores Nuestros:
Hemos leido en A Traveller's Wine Guide to Spain *que acceptan visitas del público. Estaremos en su región el día* [day] *de* [month] *de este año y nos gustaría, si es conveniente, visitar su bodega a las* [time]. *Esperamos que estarán dispuestos a recibirnos en esta fecha pero nos pondremos en contacto con ustedes por teléfono cuando llegemos a su región para confirmar nuestra visita.*

Agradeciéndoles de antemano su muy amable atención, les saluda muy atentamente

[signature]

Dear Sirs,

We have read in *A Traveller's Wine Guide to Spain* that you accept visits from the public. We will be in your area on the [day] of [month] this year and would like to visit your winery at [time]. We hope that you will be able to receive us at this time and date, but will be in contact with you by telephone to confirm our visit once we have arrived in your area.

Thanking you in advance for your kind attention.

Yours faithfully,

[signature]

Further Reading

Travel and hotel guides

Guia Campsa (revised frequently). A guide to the country's best hotels and restaurants, published by Spain's national petrol company, available in airports and bookshops in Spain. In Spanish.

Guia Oficial de Hoteles (revised frequently). A guide to Spain's hotels, Paradors and restaurants, published by the Spanish Tourist Office, available from Tourist Offices. In Spanish.

The Michelin Tourist Guide to Spain (revised frequently). Excellent for up-to-date information.

Insight Guides (APA). for a good introduction to the history and culture of the country.

The Rough Guide to Spain (Penguin U.K./Prentice Hall U.S.A.). An excellent and well-researched guide to off-beat travel in Spain.

Spanish cuisine

Andrews, Colman *Catalan Cuisine* (Headline). For an exhaustive introduction to the food of Catalonia with good recipes.

Casas, Penelope *Discovering Spain* (Alfred Knopf). Good, carefully researched general introduction to Spanish cuisine.

Sevilla, Maria José *Spain on a Plate* (BBC Books). For good recipes and an introduction to the different regional cuisines.

Torres, Marimar *The Spanish Table* (Ebury Press U.K./Doubleday U.S.A.).

More difficult to find but well worth the search is D. E. Pohren's *The Wines and Folk Food of Spain*, published by the Society of Spanish Studies (Finca Espartero, Morón de la Frontera, Sevilla, Spain) in 1972. This gives a wonderful taste of a Spain that is fast disappearing, but the book is now sadly out of date.

Spanish wines

Duiker, Hubrecht *Wines of Rioja*. Readable, detailed and well researched.

Jeffs, Julian *Sherry* (Faber & Faber). The classic work on sherry.

Millon, Marc and Kim *The Wine Roads of Spain*.

Otherwise, for up-to-date developments in the Spanish wine industry, consult the Spanish Wines Supplement published regularly by the consumer magazine *Decanter* at Priory House, 8 Battersea Park Rd, London SW8 4BG, U.K.

Writers' travel books

The following more personal and general accounts of Spain make excellent travelling companions:

Brenan, Gerald *South from Granada*, and *The Spanish Labyrinth* (Cambridge University Press). Both books are well worth reading – the first in particular is a marvellous description of village life near Granada in the 1920s and 1930s.

Hemingway, Ernest *Death in The Afternoon* (Penguin). One of the most fascinating books to have been written about Spain by an outsider, a must for anyone who is interested in bullfights.

Lee, Laurie *As I Walked Out One Midsummer's Morning*, and *A Rose for Winter* (Penguin). Beautifully written books relating the writer's travels in Spain in the 1930s and l950s, giving a lovely glimpse of the country in those two decades.

Morris, Jan *Spain* (Penguin). A favourite book of the author's, beautifully written and very readable, with wonderful descriptive passages.

Wayne, Jeremy *Lazy Days Out in Andalusia* (Cadogan Books). A sympathetic guide to Andalusia, its wines and cuisine.

Index

Page numbers in *italic* type indicate illustrations.

Index